TAKING NO PRISONERS

JOHN HARDING

TAKING NO PRISONERS

The Legend of
Frank Barson
FOOTBALL'S HARDEST MAN

First published by Pitch Publishing, 2019

Pitch Publishing
A2 Yeoman Gate
Yeoman Way
Worthing
Sussex
BN13 3QZ
www.pitchpublishing.co.uk
info@pitchpublishing.co.uk

ISBN 978 1 78531 529 9

Typesetting and origination by Pitch Publishing
Printed and bound by TJ International, Cornwall

Contents

Barson ready for action

Dedication:

To the Old Quintinians, who
also took no prisoners

Acknowledgements

TO JOYCE Woolridge for allowing me access to her PhD material and general consultation and suggestions.

To Dean Beresford for details and pictures of his Grandfather Joe Beresford, who played for Aston Villa during the 1920s and 30s.

Introduction

'I hold no brief for Barson's mentality. As a centre-half I regard him as the greatest player who has figured in English football in this position since the war.' **Steve Bloomer.**

AS THE years have gone by, Frank Barson's image in the eyes of certain football writers seems to have become ever more extreme, to such an extent that he has morphed into a comic-book character possessing thighs the width of beer barrels, a chest as hard and deep as a medieval knight's breast-plate, and a broken nose with nostrils snorting steam and flames. Rampaging across the football field snapping legs and breaking heads, he has become an early 'Iron Man', endowed with superhuman strength and durability.

The Welsh international half-back Roy Paul must bear some responsibility for starting this metallic trend. In the mid-1950s Barson was Paul's coach at Swansea City and the two men saw eye to eye where hard tackling and on-field aggression were concerned.

Paul described how it felt trying to take the ball from Barson: 'It was like trying to shift a steel girder when you tried to move the ball away, with "this tungsten-steel character's" leg pressing firmly against it.'

It's perhaps understandable that such an image has slipped into easy usage. Barson was a blacksmith, born in the 'Steel City' of Sheffield, and learned his football trade in Barnsley, a mining town where 'Iron Men' coal-cutting machines had become commonplace by the time he was born in the late 1890s.

Iron Man was not, however, a term anyone used to describe Barson in his playing days. Nor was he described as a 'hard man', in the sense that one speaks of players like Chelsea's Ron Harris, Arsenal's Peter Storey or Liverpool's Tommy Smith.

Sports academic Richard Holt has written that, 'There was a self-conscious cult of Northern aggression which applauded the violent antics of some players, with Barson being the most notorious example.' Barson, Holt claimed, 'was one of a number of hard men who were never heroes in the sense of commanding wide admiration as athletes, but there was a side of northern masculinity that admired anyone who, "could do the business". Barson was, according to Holt, only 'a hero of sorts'.

Both the modern cartoon imagery and the earnest sociological analysis completely miss the point, however.

Barson was certainly tough, but he suffered many injuries; he was from the North but never suggested his birthplace had anything to do with his success on the field; he was certainly admired as an athlete by his contemporaries but was never a 'cult' figure; yet he was quite definitely a hero to many on the terraces, a player who both thrilled and enraged football crowds throughout the 1920s.

Manchester United historian Dr Percy Young, writing in the 1960s, went so far as to claim that Barson was a 'legend in his own day', so that spectators who had never seen him knew his image before he appeared.

Harry Godwin, born in 1914 and for many years a scout with Manchester City, confirmed this: 'The first time I saw United my Dad said to me, "Which is Barson?" We didn't have programmes, the players weren't numbered in those days and I hadn't seen any of them before. But I knew which was Barson. It wasn't so much that I picked him out as that he made me pick him out. He was so obviously what everyone had told me he was, the boss of the 18 yard box, a powerful man with his hair parted straight down the middle and sleek …' (Harry Godwin, interviewed in *The Guardian*, 19 March 1980.)

Barson's footballing creed was quite simple: if you played football for a living then you had to devote yourself to it wholeheartedly; winning was as much a matter of mind as of body; pain was something you would encounter in a game that involved a great deal of physical contact; and the team was always more important than the individual. He would have slotted seamlessly into one of Bill Shankly's Liverpool 11s (and strangely enough, Barson's boyhood nickname was Shanks), the only problem being his exact position on the field of play.

As for his rumbustious reputation, Percy Young reflected: 'To the thoughtless who do not discriminate between toughness and roughness, he was a rough player. Nor did a dominant personality and an instinct for natural justice endear him to referees. If Barson was maliciously treated by an opponent he issued due warning of the wrath that was to come. He also frequently advised the referee …'

Barson's heyday was in the years before the alteration in the offside law in 1925. He was a centre-half, but not as we once knew it. He was certainly not just a defender: he was a 'pivot' around which the team 'revolved'. His post-Second World War equivalent might have been John Charles or Duncan Edwards. Today, perhaps, a combination of Roy Keane and Virgil van Dijk.

Suffice to say, he was one of the dominant football personalities of the 1920s. This small book will endeavour to explain why.

A Note on Sources:

THE 1920S are now almost a century away. Writing about a footballer who played in those far-off days is difficult but not impossible. The game was comprehensively reported in print at a time when there was little by way of radio reportage, hardly any cinema coverage and no television. The football journalists of the day performed miraculous feats of both endurance and erudition and it is upon them that this book will largely rely.

Athletic News's editor 'Tityrus' (Jimmy Catton), his successor Ivan Sharpe, plus colleagues 'Harricus' (A.H. Downs), The Seer, Brum, Cmyro, Northumbrian and Jacques; the *Lancashire Evening Post*'s 'Perseus' (John Brierly) and the *Liverpool Echo*'s 'Bee'; the *Derby Daily Telegraph*'s 'Outside Right' and the *Green 'Un*'s 'BC': these and many more unnamed toilers in the field will take us through Barson's long and eventful football journey. And it's quite a journey …

Chapter One

A Burnt Offering

'This has been a week in which one or two
surprises have come upon the football world.
Such, for instance, as the transfer of D.B.N.
Jack from Bolton Wanderers to the Arsenal
(who have spent a little fortune on their
team in recent years) and the suspension
of that great exponent of football – Frank
Barson.' **AEM Between Ourselves *Villa***
***News and Record*, 20 October 1928.**

IN JULY 1928 Frank Barson, 37-year-old ex-England, Barnsley, Aston Villa and Manchester United centre-back, signed for Watford of the Football League Third Division South on a free transfer. On 29 September (a day after penicillin was discovered), eight games into the season, Watford entertained Fulham. Late in the first half trouble ensued, witnessed by the *Sporting Life* football correspondent:

Exactly how the situation arose it would be difficult to say – things happen so quickly in football. But with the centre of play some fifteen yards away I saw Barson and Temple, the Fulham outside-right, spinning round apparently locked together. Temple was clinging to Barson round the thighs and the Watford man was striving to free himself. Barson obviously annoyed by Temple's refusal to release himself, lifted his arm into what the police would call a 'striking attitude'. Before any blow could or would have been struck, however, other players came between the pair.

Now the referee, Mr W.E. Russell of Swindon, was following the play and could not have been a witness to the incident. He at once went across to the linesman on that side of the ground and, presumably acting on what was told him, ordered Barson off. Barson argued his case in vain and though Barrett the Fulham captain added his entreaties, the referee stood his ground. Opinion was unanimous on the ground at the time that the other party was the aggressor.[1]

Watford supporter Mr C.T. Edgar of Railway Cottages, Hatch End, claimed he saw the incident and that Barson was not wholly to blame: 'I say he has been most unfairly dealt with.' On the other hand, a Fulham supporter, 'Veritas' of Maida Vale, who said the incident took place directly in front of him, declared that, 'it was significant that the home supporters, who outnumbered the Fulham supporters by about 50 to 1, were silent and there was not the slightest demonstration against the referee.'[2]

Within a few days, a petition was drawn up, arranged by the Mayor of Watford, Alderman T. Rushton, who felt that Barson had been unfairly treated: 'My view is that Temple caught hold of Barson's leg and as far as I could see Barson was endeavouring to get his leg released when the referee ordered him off the field. I did not see Barson kick Temple unless he kicked him in trying to release his leg.'[3]

The petition was signed by some 5,000 Watford fans and letters from fans started to appear in newspapers, all generally supportive. A *Daily Herald* reader wrote, 'I was booked off duty and went along with a Willesden friend to see a match in which Watford took part. This was the only time I had seen Barson play. Both my friend and I were neutral but it appeared to us that Barson touched an opponent and a free kick was given against him. I should think this happened at least half a dozen times. When an opponent was to blame no action was taken. On one occasion a whistle was blown for a foul and both teams and spectators expected it was in favour of Watford but to the surprise of everybody it was given against Barson. What surprised me most was the fact that Barson always came up smiling instead of losing his temper as he easily might have done in the circumstances.'[4]

Football Association Secretary Frederick Wall was immediately contacted and agreed to meet Rushton some days later. Wall commented, 'I know nothing about a petition. There have been petitions from time to time but I don't recall whether they had reference to cases of men being sent off the field.'[5]

On 16 October, however, it was announced that Barson would be suspended for the rest of the season, a 'savage' sentence that Barson protested would impoverish him: 'I have a wife and three children and am faced with the prospect of seven months without a livelihood.'

Barson gave his own account of the incident to a reporter the next day:

'What exactly happened was this: Temple got hold of my left leg and persisted in holding it for between 15 and 20 seconds for which the referee gave the Watford team a foul. It was some five seconds after the whistle blew before I managed to free my leg. *I hopped round on one leg trying to get the other free.* The referee seemed in doubt and consulted the linesman, following which he came over and ordered me off the field *apparently thinking I had been trying to kick Temple.* The Fulham captain, Barrett, came up and told the referee that I could not be sent off the field, as I had done nothing, but he was ordered away. I understood that Temple informed the Football Association that he was not kicked by me. I asked to be given a hearing but this was refused.'[6]

As the confusions and outrage mounted, the question arose: what had happened to the petition signed by Watford fans and presented by the Mayor? Alderman Rushton thought it inadvisable not to say anything regarding the matter: 'The player has been suspended for the rest of the season,' he said, 'and the penalty is certainly sufficient for any offence he may have committed.'[7]

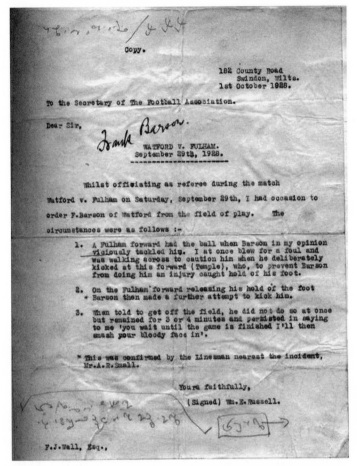

Copy.

182 County Road
Swindon, Wilts.
1st October 1928.

To the Secretary of The Football Association.

Dear Sir,

Frank Barson.

WATFORD V. FULHAM.
September 29th, 1928.

Whilst officiating as referee during the match
Watford v. Fulham on Saturday, September 29th, I had occasion to
order F.Barson of Watford from the field of play.   The
circumstances were as follows :-

1. A Fulham forward had the ball when Barson in my opinion
    viciously tackled him. I at once blew for a foul and
    was walking across to caution him when he deliberately
    kicked at this forward (Temple), who, to prevent Barson
    from doing him an injury caught hold of his foot.

2. On the Fulham forward releasing his hold of the foot
    * Barson then made a further attempt to kick him.

3. When told to get off the field, he did not do so at once
    but remained for 3 or 4 minutes and persisted in saying
    to me 'you wait until the game is finished I'll then
    smash your bloody face in'.

* This was confirmed by the Lineman nearest the incident,
    Mr.A.R.Small.

Yours faithfully,

(Signed) Wm.E.Russell.

F.J.Wall, Esq.,

Referee's report

All would be revealed, however, a week later when
Frederick Wall was interviewed. When Mayor Rushton
arrived at the FA offices on 12 October, Wall had rather
disingenuously asked him why he had come.

'He said he had come to present a petition on behalf
of Barson and he asked if he might read it. I said, "Before
doing so, I think it right to ask you whether you have seen
the referee's report with reference to Barson."

'He said he had not. I showed him the original report [see illustration].

'It read:

A Fulham forward had the ball when in my opinion Barson viciously tackled him. I at once blew for a foul and was walking across to caution him when he deliberately kicked at this forward (Temple) who, to prevent Barson from doing him an injury caught hold of his foot. On the Fulham forward releasing his hold of the foot Barson made a further attempt to kick him. *

When told to get off the field he did not do so at once but remained for three or four minutes and persisted in saying, 'Wait until the game is finished I'll then smash your bloody face in.' (signed by the referee)

*This was confirmed by the Linesman nearest the incident, Mr A.R. Small.

'"Do you know," Wall asked the Mayor, "anything of Barson's history as a football player?"

'The Mayor said he did not. I [then] read him information showing we – the FA – had had to consider numerous reports on Barson's misconduct on the field; that he had been suspended on three previous occasions, once for a month, and twice for three months and reported three times for misconduct while playing for the Watford club.

'I then asked the Mayor what he proposed to do.

'He said, "Well, Mr Wall, I will not ask you to receive the petition."

'I said, "You have taken the right course. I feel that you have been placed in an invidious position."

_ 'The Mayor said, "I don't want to carry the petition away with me. Will you destroy it?"

'I destroyed the petition with his knowledge and approval.

'Was it burned?' asked the interviewer.

'It was burned in his presence,' Wall said.[8]

Suitably chastened, the Mayor headed back home. Meanwhile, Frederick Wall proceeded to reduce to ashes what was left of Barson's football career.

Charles Buchan, the newly retired Arsenal forward, wrote: 'I am extremely sorry to learn of Frank Barson's suspension. At this time of his career, for Barson has been playing for a good number of seasons, it may have serious consequences for it will be difficult to resume after such an enforced rest. In fact, it may mean the end of his playing days ...'[9]

Endnotes
1. *Sporting Life*, 29 September 1928
2. *Daily Herald*, 19 October 1928
3. *The Scotsman*, 10 October 1928
4. *Daily Herald*, 16 October 1928
5. *Dundee Courier*, 10 October 1928
6. *Derby Daily Telegraph*, 16 October 1928
7. *Dundee Courier*, Wednesday, 17 October 1928
8. *Derby Daily Telegraph*, 25 October 1928
9. *Watford Observer*, 20 October 1928

Chapter Two

Sheffield

'The other evening my new comrade Albert Pape, the centre-forward, asked me what I should have been if I had not become a footballer.

"A blacksmith," I replied.

'Pape laughed. He thought it was a joke. But it is a fact. Not the village blacksmith – but a Sheffield blacksmith.' **The Truth About My Football Troubles, *Thomson's Weekly News*, 2 May 1925 (Thereafter 'Mems').**

IN 1727 the novelist and travel-writer Daniel Defoe wrote: 'This town of Sheffield is very populous and large, the streets narrow, and the houses dark and black, occasioned by the continued smoke of the forges, which are always at work. Here they make all sorts of cutlery-ware, but especially that of edged-tools, knives, razors, axes and nails; and here the only mill of the sort, which was in use in England for some time was set up, (viz.) for turning their grindstones, though now 'tis grown more common.'[1]

Over 150 years later, Alfred Gatty described how Sheffield had changed: once when looking down into the Don Valley, 'the eye traversed a rich and extended scene of agricultural interest and beauty.' An ancient wood, Hall Carr Wood, clothed the hillside above the village of Attercliffe and beyond, the church spire of Laughton-en-le-Morthen and the church tower of Handsworth, were distinctly visible through the clear atmosphere with Treeton and Whiston in the intervening distance.

Now, however, 'The wood has disappeared, cottages have sprung up on the hillside, and down in the valley, where the railway shoots its straight line beside the meandering Don, there stands, as it were, Dante's city of Dis: masses of buildings, from the tops of which issue fire, and smoke, and steam, which cloud the whole scene, however bright the sunshine.'[2]

The transformation had been largely wrought by technical innovations such as newer, swifter processes for producing steel invented by Bessemer that helped major firms to establish Sheffield as a centre for heavy engineering, shifting the emphasis away from the traditional lighter trades such as edge tools and cutlery.

The new heavy industry plants were built on 'green field' sites in the wide River Don valley to the east of Sheffield itself, in the neighbouring villages of Brightside, Attercliffe (the 'East End' of Sheffield) and finally Grimesthorpe, where Frank Barson was born in April 1891.

There was a constant supply of water from the River Don and railway access to the coking coal from local collieries and to pig iron from the continent. The flat land beside the Don afforded the construction and subsequent expansion of large industrial sites so that by the 1890s there had arisen a solid mass of works and railway sidings surrounded by rows and rows of terraced houses, principally along Sheffield's Carlisle Street and Savile Street. Here were situated Charles Cammell's Cyclops Works, John Brown's Atlas Works (both named appropriately after giants of Greek mythology) and Thomas Firth's Norfolk Works, with the railways running beside and between them. Workers had been attracted from all over the British Isles.

The first Barson family had arrived in Sheffield in the 1850s. Frank's grandfather William, born in Derby to a poor family, his father a frame worker, initially worked as a groom and in 1851 was living in Bag Lane, Derby, with his wife Mary Ann (nee Camp), a dressmaker from Leicester whose father had been an agricultural labourer. They had three children at that point: Elizabeth, George and Thomas.

William had been drawn by the prospect of more prosperous work, which was typical of the many workers drawn into Sheffield during the middle years of the 19th century. By the first decade of the 20th century Sheffield's population had grown from 135,310 in 1851 to 380,793 in 1901, or well over 400,000 if newly incorporated areas are added. Many of these workers were, like Barson, new to the steel and coal trades – migrants from the surrounding countryside and beyond, including many from Ireland.

By 1861 William was working as a labourer at the Cyclops Steel Works in Brightside and living in a back-to-back at 21 Sutherland Street, Burngreave. In that same year, his eldest son George, aged 13, was already employed in the nearby rolling mill. Thomas was an errand boy and William, Frank's father, was just two years old. Four years on, however, everything changed.

On 11 March 1864 there occurred what became known as the Great Sheffield Flood, also known as the Great Inundation, a disaster that devastated areas in and above the city. At about midnight, the Dale Dyke Dam at Bradfield, one of four reservoirs built about eight miles north-west of Sheffield and planned to supply the developing steel industry, collapsed, releasing a torrent of water that ultimately killed some 250 people. It also devastated an area that stretched from the Dam itself, down the Loxley Valley, through Malin Bridge and Hillsborough, into Sheffield town centre and beyond, ultimately reaching Sutherland Street, where the Barson family lived.

In the disaster's aftermath, a special Act of Parliament was passed to enable compensation to be paid to those who had suffered damage to property, injury to persons, and loss of life – one of the largest insurance awards of its time. A three-man commission, under William Overend QC, worked their way through 6,500 claims, eventually awarding some £273,988. The claimants represented a remarkable cross section of the town's population, from the poorest and most lowly to the wealthy and enterprising, and their stories were frequently distressing and tragic in the extreme: sole survivors of large families, the permanently crippled, the orphaned and widowed. Sometimes the stories were dishonest and occasionally ludicrous, and sadly the Barson family's claims fell into this category.

Their home (or rather, two rooms) in Sutherland Street was at the furthest extent of the flood, but they were still eligible to make an application, as overflowing river water had caused a lot of collateral damage to buildings and property. In fact, 60 houses and basements had been flooded in Sutherland Street.

The first part of William Barson's claim was simple enough and consisted of a list of items damaged by or lost in the water, and a sorry list it was: viz. Maiden & Pot, Bread, Pot and Bread, two Panshons, Rabbit, Frying Pan, Clothes Horse, New Pair of Boots and other articles. These came to £3 12s. There was then the 'Cleaning House, Cellars and Furniture, which came to 12s.' The total came to £4 4s. The adjudication panel awarded them just £2 5s, somewhat typical, as most small claims were reduced almost automatically.

What followed was more problematic. William Barson suffered from rheumatic fever and inflammation of the liver, but he tried to prove that his worsening health was a direct consequence of the flood and claimed injury compensation of £200. Sadly, he died in the months before the case came to adjudication. Thus, Mary Ann proceeded to put in a claim for compensation for the loss of the family breadwinner, 'being wife or husband of the deceased person or his or her parent or child as defined in 9 and 10 Victoria C.93'. (This was the Fatal Accidents Act 1846, commonly known as Lord Campbell's Act, which allowed relatives of people killed by the wrongdoing of others to recover damages.) The Barson family at that time consisted of Mary Ann herself, then aged 46, Elizabeth, aged 18, George, aged 16, Thomas, aged 14, William, aged 6, Jane, aged 3, and Frederick, aged 4 months.

Mary Ann put in a claim for £500 – but was awarded just £5. Frank Barson would often recall the bitterness that the family continued to feel at the paltry amount awarded to a widow and six children. 'How were they supposed to survive on £5?' he would ask. 'It was a terrific struggle and I often wondered how they managed.' It looked to someone like Barson, in retrospect, like a grave injustice. 'It made me angry just to contemplate it ...'

The official explanation for the parsimonious nature of many of the awards was that although Overend and his colleagues, 'were deeply moved by the wretchedness of such cases,' and much as they sympathised with the bereaved, they were empowered to award only 'the pecuniary loss' sustained. If, for example, a father claimed for the death of a son, it was necessary to ascertain how much that son had been earning and how much financially he had benefitted the father.

What adds to the tragedy of this whole situation is that the Relief Committee found themselves in the embarrassing position of having almost half of the original monies donated to relieve distress *left over* so that it had to be returned to the donors, and £8,000 given to local hospitals. Clearly, the committee could have been far less miserly towards those whose lives had been devastated on that terrible night of 11 March 1864.

In the Barson case, however, it looked like the committee simply didn't believe Mary Ann's story.

The family survived, of course, and by 1871 they had moved a mile further out to Grimesthorpe, to 36 Bland Street, close by the Grimesthorpe Cammell Lairds works.

George was now a 'spring fitter' and Thomas a labourer, plus there was a lodger, a 'hammer driver' called Alfred Easthorpe who would soon marry Mary Ann. Their neighbours included a 'puddler', several labourers, railway spring fitters, iron workers, a hammer driver, a shopkeeper, a school mistress, a coalminer, and an engine smith hailing variously from Derby, Wolverhampton, Newcastle, Gateshead, Stafford, Nottingham, Herefordshire, and Norfolk. Almost everyone worked for Cammell Laird.

The Barsons would ultimately multiply, Frank's uncles and an aunt producing between them some 17 cousins, the majority of whom continued to live in streets surrounding the Cammell Laird works, the men almost invariably working for the eponymous steel firm.

Frank's Aunt Elizabeth would escape the immediate area, however, when she married a porter called Thomas Rhoads Beavin in 1881, who became a fruiterer, then a greengrocer and eventually a fruit dealer, living in 25 Barretta Street, Pitsmoor. (Pitsmoor was described as 'eminently respectable and a languorous and soothing suburb', in an article in the *Sheffield Daily Telegraph* in

MR. GEORGE BARSON.

DEATH OF WELL-KNOWN SHEFFIELD MAN.

A well-known personality in the district will be missed in the death of Mr. George Barson, of 73, Firth Park road, Sheffield, who died on Saturday, aged 81.

Commencing work at Messrs. Cammell Laird and Co., as a boy in the spring department, Grimesthorpe, he became a skilled workman, foreman and manager of the department in turn.

He retired after 57 years' service with the firm 11 years ago, at the age of 70. All his working career was spent with them, and on his retirement a presentation was made to him.

Mr. Barson. A reader of the "Sheffield Independent" for well over half a century, he was a staunch Liberal in politics. Mr. Barson was also a Wesleyan, and was one of the original trustees of the Grimesthorpe Wesleyan Reform Chapel.

He was born in Derby, but came to Sheffield as a boy, and had lived practically all the time in the Pitsmoor district.

WEDNESDAY SUPPORTER.

Married 59 years, he leaves a widow, aged 79, seven sons and daughters, and several grandchildren and great-grandchildren.

A shareholder and keen supporter of the Wednesday F.C. for many years, he remembered seeing the brothers Clegg play in the club's early days. He is the uncle of Frank Barson, the ex-International footballer.

Death of George Barson

1906, the people living in the area consisting of doctors, teachers, shopkeepers and business men.)

Uncle Thomas was not so fortunate. He worked in the Cammell Laird workshops as a railway 'spring fitter', living alongside Frank's father William in Bland Street before moving to nearby Margate Street, where he died in 1894 – but not before producing five children.

Frank's Uncle George would be the most prolific, however, and by far the most successful. His story was one of hard work and deserved rewards. Born in 1848, in employment from the age of 13, and working for Cammell Laird all his life, he rose from being a simple 'workman' to becoming a foreman and ultimately a manager of the Grimesthorpe Cammell Laird spring department. It's no surprise that so many of his relatives would find work in that particular department as he had control over the hiring and firing of men. He also became one of the most prominent citizens of the area, being a staunch Liberal in politics and a lifelong Wesleyan.

In all, George worked for Cammell's for 57 years and when retiring aged 70 he was given a suitably lavish presentation. During those years he had gradually moved himself and his family away from the meaner streets of Grimesthorpe. From Hunsley Street, close to where he was brought up, thence to Owler Lane and eventually to the prosperous Firth Park Road in Pitsmoor, his was a steady rise, taking his eight children along with him.

When he died in 1930, having lived 82 years, his funeral (along with a photograph) was prominently reported in various local papers. At the service held at the Grimesthorpe Wesleyan Reform Chapel were seven sons and daughters, several grandchildren and various great grandchildren, as well as representatives of the English Steel Corporation, the Grimesthorpe works and local politicians, while the service itself was conducted by W.H. Vaughan, Wesleyan National President. Notable by their absence at the funeral, or at least not worthy of notice, were all of Frank Barson's family.

Some years later, on the death of George's wife, a property portfolio consisting of some 20 houses in the Firth Park and Grimesthorpe area was auctioned. George Barson was thus a prosperous man by the time of his death.

The fate of George's younger brother William, Frank's father, would be dramatically different, although initially his progress would follow traditional Barson lines.

In 1881 he was working at the Cammell Laird works as a fireman but would marry a Dudley-born girl, Agnes, the daughter of a coalminer living in nearby Moss Street. The couple would move a street away to Carlisle Road where, on 11 April 1891, Frank Barson was born. They would move once more the following year to Draper Street, which would remain the family home for decades to come. At this point, having been an 'engine tenter stationary' (a man who tends a stationary machine), William was working in his brother's spring-making workshop, having fathered six children.

In his *Thomson's Weekly News* lifestory, Frank would write: 'At the age of 13, I commenced work. I would not swing the lead at any time but I fancied swinging the hammer so I was apprenticed to a blacksmith. One Monday morning I started my duties at the great Sheffield Cammell Laird engineering works ... my wage was 5s 7d a week ...'

He added, 'My father died about this time and my mother required all the assistance that her sons could give.'[3]

There was, however, slightly more to the story than that.

Endnotes

1. Daniel Defoe, *A tour thro' the whole island of Great Britain, divided into circuits or journeys* (London: JM Dent and Co, 1927)
2. Alfred Gatty, *Sheffield: past and present* (1873)
3. Mems

Chapter Three

Grimesthorpe

*'I was born at Grimesthorpe on the outskirts
of Sheffield in April 1891.'* **Mems.**

*'Old-fashioned sports were revived this
week at the Grimesthorpe Feast by Mr
Herbert Smith, of the Victoria Hotel,
Grimesthorpe. It is over 20 years since the
greasy pole was part of the sports there.
On the first night there were 30 entrants
for a ham weighing 15lbs, and after
climbing a pole 30ft high a boy named
William Heard, 11 years of age, won.'*
**Sheffield Daily Telegraph, Saturday,
13 July 1912.**

GRIMESTHORPE VILLAGE is ancient, a Dark
Ages farmstead settlement built on an embankment,
enjoying expansive and open views in all directions

across the lower Don Valley. *Drake's Road Book* of 1825 described it thus:

> The appearance of this village from the railway, when it first bursts upon the sight, is exceedingly striking and partakes in some degree of the grotesque. The most conspicuous object is the blackened brick building of the Grimesthorpe Grinding Wheel Company; the village lies beyond and around it rise high hills which have been invested with a somewhat romantic air by the extensive quarrying operations to which they have been subjected. The lofty hill in which the excavations appear, and whose bold brow is shaded with wood, is the classic Wincobank, of which Sheffield bards have often sung and on which they say: 'the golden cheek of eve rests loveliest…'

By the time Barson was born, however, the village had become a suburb of Sheffield and was dominated, smothered you could say, by the Cammell Laird steelworks sprawling along the valley floor below.

Items from the local paper in the month of Frank's birth seem to confirm the 'grim' element of its name: a 'lad' named Harry Proctor was sentenced to 12 strokes with a birch rod for stealing and disposing of seven pigeons; an 'engine tenter' died after falling from a ladder at Cammell's works; four young men were fined 14s and 6d each for playing pitch and toss in the street; and a labourer aged 63 hung himself from his bed-post with a leather waist belt after receiving bad news from his doctor. Five years after Frank's birth, in 1896, his father William was summonsed, along with 13 other Grimesthorpe working men, for aiding and abetting a prize fight held in nearby Woolley Woods. Grimesthorpe was a tough place to grow up in.

The serried rows of terraced housing built in their thousands after 1864 to accommodate the Cammell workers as the steel industry expanded north-eastwards along the Don valley were hardly salubrious dwellings, but even so were a cut above the older back-to-backs where Barson's father had first lived when arriving in Brightside as a child in 1859. The Sutherland Street dwellings had consisted of a cellar, a living room-cum-kitchen, a first floor bedroom and an attic. Three of the four walls of each back-to-back were common with adjoining houses and only one wall, either facing the street or the yard, was free and broken by windows and a door. The back-to-backs were built around courts with the entrances to those houses that had their doors in the courtyard being through passages, locally called 'jennels', built under first-floor rooms, hence the address 'back of ... etc.'

In Grimesthorpe, by contrast, the artisan houses where Frank and his family were to spend a large part of their lives were superior 'bye-law' terrace houses, with front and back doors and through ventilation. Bricks for building them were in great demand, as reflected in neighbouring circular Grimesthorpe brickworks, whose constant fumes only added to the ubiquitous air-born pollution.

Superior housing or not, the branch of the Barson family headed by William was hard-working but usually hard-up. 'There used to be a joke amongst the brothers Barson – the best-dressed brother was the one who was first astir in the morning,' Frank later quipped.

He was the third of five brothers: William, George, Ewart and Sydney being the others, Sarah, Blanch and Nora the sisters. All but Nora would work and raise families within a few hundred yards of the street where they were born. All the men would labour, as did their father and uncles before them, for Cammell Laird.

Like many of the families of tool and steel artisans resident in the Grimesthorpe streets, Barson's was an extended family – both horizontally and vertically – whose residential and occupational stability lasted throughout the 19th century and well until the 1920s. Frank himself would still be living in Carlisle Street in the mid-1920s, despite his relative affluence as a professional footballer.

The significance of the family as a social support unit consisted of flexible combinations of nuclear families within the same yards, of extended families within the same streets, and of working groups inside the same families. Thus, it helped that Uncle George was manager of a department of the Cammell works that specialised in railway machinery, upon which many of the Barson's worked.

Frank's father was an 'engineer' (or strictly an engine tenter, that is, someone who 'tended' or oversaw the operation of a stationary steam engine that drove a line shaft, driving factory machinery within a works, the term 'tenter' being a corruption of the word attendant).

Frank's elder brother William would be a railway 'spring vice-man' (the springs being key to the hydraulic system supporting the weight of railway carriages) and 'spring maker' and he lived in Draper Street all his life.

Brother George would be a labourer in the Cammell Laird foundry and lived a few streets away in Hawkshead Road. Brother Ewart would 'make good' and eventually become a foreman for a general builders, and move out to Fairbank Road, a leafier suburb half a mile away. Youngest brother Sydney would remain on Carlisle Road as a furnace man (and regularly find himself in trouble).

Frank's sister Sarah would marry an examiner of steel castings and also stay on Carlisle Road, as would his sister Blanch, who married a 'blacksmith striker', an assistant whose job it was to swing a large sledgehammer in heavy forging operations, as directed by the blacksmith. Only sister Nora would move away. Following a term as a domestic servant in 1911, she met and married a colliery worker and moved to Abertillery in Wales.

Barson's close-knit and close-by family (for there were also uncles and aunts living within a mile or so) would be one of the principal reasons why he would find it so difficult to leave Grimesthorpe in later years, even when such stubbornness threatened to place his football career in jeopardy.

What's more, the factory they lived so close to would dominate their lives both when working and resting. The large industrial firms of the city played a significant role in organising worker's leisure, and Cammell was no exception. Families such as Barson's took their leisure increasingly inside the factory premises, where canteens and organised sport competitions attracted them during the weekends.

The Cammell Laird Sports Club was founded in 1910 and its commodious pavilion would be opened at Shiregreen in 1912, with the chairman and managing directors of the company presiding. In 1914 a Grand Fete Day was held at Shiregreen, with 4,000 of the company's families and workers attending. The Grimesthorpe Prize Band played, there were Punch and Judy shows and coconut shies, as well as bowling matches and a tug-of-war contest between various departments of the Cammell Laird works. All the contestants were presented with a silver matchbox each, while tea was served to about 1,500 children, each of whom received a box of Rowntrees chocolates.

The Cammell Laird chairman gave a speech and emphasised that, 'Their object was to meet in a friendly and social way from time to time when they could get to know each other better, for he felt that half the disputes which arose were due to ignorance and misunderstanding ... On the sports-ground they met as Englishmen and sportsmen, the only difference between one man and another being a difference of skill in the various games they played.'[1]

Frank's cousin George, son of Uncle George, was a keen cricketer and footballer, and he played a large part in organising the day. He would regularly officiate at the club's AGMs and 'smoker' concerts and even instituted a Barson Shield, to be awarded to the best Cammell Laird football player annually.

On a more practical note, at certain factories in Grimesthorpe and the surrounding villages the entire workforce collectively farmed in the fields enclosed in the factories' premises and supplemented their industrial wages with the sale of agricultural produce in times of economic need. During seasonal industrial downturns, allotments scattered in between workers' houses provided those who worked them, according to statistics of the time, with up to one-fourth of the foodstuffs they consumed. Well into the 1930s, in fact, Seebohm Rowntree's study of budgets in 1931 revealed that gardens and allotments could provide a quarter of the food consumed by families. However, allotments and even fishing – back then possibly in the River Don – were not to be confused with the middle-class pursuits of gardening and angling. For working men they had a serious purpose beyond that of simple relaxation. (Significantly, however, in later life, fishing would be Frank Barson's principal leisure-time occupation.)

Frank had little to say about his early childhood, however, that wasn't related to his future football career. School was clearly not a priority: 'I regret to say that I missed my studies at school for this love of a ball and sometimes an old tin can if a ball were not procurable; and I regret that on many occasions I invoked the wrath of my parents for I used to return home with damaged boots and torn trousers.'[2]

He attended Grimesthorpe Council School, opened in 1875 by Sir John Brown, one of Sheffield's self-made millionaire industrialists. (Ironically, in 1848 it had been Brown who'd invented the conical steel spring buffer for railway carriages, which he sold to various railway companies throughout the UK and upon which so many of the Barson family were to labour to produce in the succeeding decades.)

Barson would be the sole Old Boy of any distinction, apart from a Sir Tom Percival, clerk of Tyneside Board of Guardians, who would endow the school with a library in 1930. Barson would leave no such endowments; he didn't even represent the school at his favourite sport.

'Strange enough to relate,' he wrote, 'I did not figure in the school teams.' Although perhaps, not so strange: 'Our home circumstances did not permit the purchase of football togs. Until I was over 12 years of age I had never donned a jersey. I was usually in the thick of a kick and rush for a small ball in the playground, and on numerous occasions I have played the truant in order to join in scratch games played by all sorts and sizes of boys and youths on neighbouring waste pieces of ground. I liked to be in the thick of the fray and it almost goes without saying that no power on earth would make me go into goal! So there were punishments for me at home and at school and often there was severe usage of me on the field of play.'[3]

Whatever academic studies he might subsequently have undertaken, however, were to be ended abruptly in 1904. In mid-August of that year Frank's father killed himself. One paper reported the shattering event thus:

SUICIDE DOUBLY SECURE

On the Thursday morning a fitter employed by Vickers and Son went to the firm's private reservoir at Wincobank Hill to take the state of the water. On the bank he found a man's coat and hat. The coat had bloodstains on the front and when he picked it up a pocket-book fell out of the top pocket. In this book was written plainly on two pages the deceased man's name and address. In another pocket was found a blood-stained knife wrapped in a piece of rag.

Police were called and the reservoir was dragged.

After some time, several hours, the body of the deceased was brought to the surface and it was then seen that his throat was severely cut. [One report suggested there was 'a fearful gash in his windpipe being almost cut through'.] Despite this horrible injury, William Barson had still managed to climb a fence of boards 10ft in height in order to get to the water where he had drowned.[4, 5]

A verdict of 'suicide during a fit of temporary insanity' was returned, being the usual legal fiction that avoided the fact that suicide was still then technically a crime.

Barson senior was part of a sad national trend: suicide rates in males had steadily increased in the UK from the mid-19th century, to reach a peak of 30.3 per 100,000 by 1905. What's more, taking one's life was not an uncommon event in Grimesthorpe. There had been recent cases in Bland Street, where the Barsons lived, in the adjacent Carlisle Road, and also up on Wincobank. The reasons were various and not necessarily related to grinding poverty, although it was usually closely associated with being underprivileged: depression, drink, bankruptcy, fear of debilitating illness. The method was usually crude, often similar to William Barson's, involving cutting one's own throat, or even drowning

SUICIDE DOUBLY SECURE.

What appears to be a very determined case of suicide has occurred at Wincobank. On Thursday morning a fitter employed by Messrs Vickers, Sons, and Maxim went up to their private reservoir, which supplies the works, and which is situated near to Wincobank Wood. Close to the water's edge he found a man's hat and coat. The coat had bloodstains on the front of it, and in the pocket, wrapped in a blood-stained piece of handkerchief, was a knife closed up, and also covered with blood.

Information was given to the police, and constables, after several hours' work, recovered the body of a man named William Barson, of Grimesthorpe, who until about three weeks ago was employed by Messrs Cammell, Laird, and Co., as an engine tenter. His throat had a fearful gash in it his windpipe being almost cut through. The reservoir is surrounded by a hoarding about ten feet in height, and this he would have to scale to get to the water.

The deceased, who was 46 years of age, leaves a widow and a large family. He had been out of work for three weeks, and this had made him very depressed, with the result that he drank somewhat heavily.

Barson's father's death

in a reservoir. None, however, combined scaling a high fence with throat cutting and *then* drowning. One has to wonder how William Barson managed it. It's often said that suicide shares with accidental death the qualities of 'suddenness, unexpectedness, and violence'. That was certainly the case with William Barson.

At the inquest into William's death, Frank's elder brother William Jnr stated unequivocally that, 'his father had never threatened to commit suicide'. Thus, no one could be blamed for missing the signs. There were, it seems, mitigating circumstances. It was revealed that the unfortunate man had been unemployed for a month after spraining his back, 'and since then had been drinking heavily'.

Whether this was because he was afraid of losing his job is unknown but seems unlikely, however, given that his brother was manager of the section where William was employed, that they were on good terms and that Barson had not been sacked.

There is often a tendency to look for a scapegoat following a suicide. The surviving spouse, parents or even child may be blamed for not seeing the signs of the impending suicide or for not meeting the needs of the deceased. However, William Jnr went on to reveal that his father, 'was in the habit of having periodical bouts of drinking which would last about a month'.[6] Life in the Barson household prior to the suicide cannot have been easy, therefore.

There was another complicating factor for young Frank to deal with. The decision to call suicide an 'accident' or to attribute it to an illness in order to protect a child from the truth is common. In this case, however, there was no chance of concealment or ambiguity. The death was reported in gory detail in a number of regional newspapers and was thus a public event. Grimesthorpe was still essentially a village and there would be no chance that such news could be concealed for more than an hour or so.

Bereavement following the suicide of a family member has been called a 'personal and interpersonal disaster'. It generates horror, anger, shame, confusion and guilt –

feelings that a child can experience as overwhelming. The feelings of abandonment and rejection may be irrational but following a suicide they are almost universal: 'He could not have loved me; he did not think I was worth living for.'

Exactly how young Frank Barson reacted to all this is hard to tell (in three subsequent sets of reminiscences he never mentioned it), although a great deal of his subsequent behaviour may well be traced back to this particular moment in time. It certainly cannot be overlooked as a factor in his subsequent career. Delinquency has been found to correlate with parental bereavement, particularly in adolescents, loss generating anti-social behaviour: petty theft, car-stealing, fights, drug-taking, or testing of authority systems. It wouldn't be long before the young Frank Barson began kicking against authority's traces.

One also has to wonder how the event played out in the wider Barson family, given that William's brother, Frank's Uncle George, was a leading light in local Reform Methodist circles and one of the original trustees of the Grimesthorpe Wesleyan Reform Chapel, one of the centres of Grimesthorpe life. One of Charles Wesley's less attractive moments came when he wrote that the bodies of the men and women who had killed themselves should be hung from chains in public places. As late as 1898 the *Wesleyan Methodist Magazine* claimed suicide levels had increased by 25 per cent since 1893 and that the suicidal 'ideation' derived from the same 'disgusted despair which prompts the savage to self-slaughter'.

In the meantime, it would have been particularly sad for the young Frank that his father took his life up on

Wincobank Hill, a wooded expanse that had served as a wild and unofficial adventure playground for Frank and his friends, who would spend days on end up there following streams, climbing trees and trapping birds and rabbits. Wincobank Wood was an exhilarating release from the smoke, dirt and hard labour just below.

In 1826, Ebenezer Rhodes visited it for his book on 'Yorkshire Scenery' and found that 'from whatever point of elevation Sheffield is beheld, Wincobank appears above all steep surrounding objects, and the woods that clothe its acclivities and ornament its brow give this noble eminence a grand and imposing character.'[7]

His father's death, however, ended those carefree days: 'One Monday morning I started my duties at the great Sheffield Cammell Laird engineering works ... my wage was 5s 7d a week ...'[8]

Perhaps, however, we can trace some kind of deeper inspiration born of those early Wincobank Hill days in Frank's later career. It boasts an Iron Age hill fort considered to be the first step along a set of fortifications called the Roman Rig, thought to have been constructed by the Celtic Brigantes tribe as part of a 1st-century defensive line built in an attempt to halt the northward advance of the Roman legions.

What's more, the Brigantes themselves were a warlike race who did not flinch from any battle, nor scorn any excuse to take up arms against any opponent, no matter how small the issue ...

Endnotes

1. *Liverpool Echo*, 15 June 1914
2. Mems
3. Ditto
4. *Hull Daily Mail*, 12 August 1904
5. Ditto
6. *Sheffield Daily Telegraph*, 16 August 1904
7. *Yorkshire Scenery, pt. i.* London, 1826
8. Mems

Chapter Four

Football Beginnings

'I donned my first jersey when I was nearly 13 years of age. How can I ever forget it? It was zebra in colour and I wore blue knickers and a cheap pair of real football boots. We were not all zebra-like in appearance. We were a team of many colours. My colours were my own fancy.' **Mems.**

'For weeks and months, perhaps, I had been watched on the field of play by the keen eyes of club scouts but I had never heard that I was under observation. And if I had been told so I would not have believed it. It was beyond my wildest dreams that I could become a professional footballer.' **Mems.**

FRANK BARSON'S first football team was called 'The Albion', not to be confused with one of the original members of the Sheffield FA in 1877. Barson's Albion was for local Grimesthorpe boys. 'A leading light in the organisation of these competitions was Mr Joe Lumby, who kept an ice-cream shop in Grimesthorpe. It had always been his desire to encourage football in the district. I paid two shillings to join the Albion, and being a big lad and one who always spoke his mind I declared that I thought my position should be at centre-half.'

The Albion competed in the locality in various medal competitions for boys between the ages of 11 and 13. They carried the necessary goalposts along to each match: 'Each member of the team took his turn in conveying the posts – kept in some convenient backyard – to the various playing pitches. The team did well considering that the players were not coached. Sometimes we got a bit rough if things were not going our way on the field.'

It was at this time that Barson realised that he could head the ball with some skill. 'I was often described as, "India-rubber neck" but very soon I got a nickname which stuck to me all the time I figured in junior football. I was a tall, lanky lad and they called me "Shanks" and as "Shanks" I soon got a reputation.'

He admitted many years later that even as a youngster he was sometimes 'too enthusiastic' and that even then referees paid close attention to him. He also felt that the opposition tended to target him, perhaps with a view to upsetting him and getting him into trouble. It was clear evidence of a quick temper and an inherent tendency to confront authority, often for what appeared to others as trivial reasons. It would be a common theme throughout his career.

In those days, however, and particularly at junior level, referees tended to take the easy option if things got difficult: 'On one occasion I remember we were playing a Hillsborough team. The game was strenuous. The referee did not please us. Decisions were disputed. Fortunately for the referee the trams were passing the playing pitch. Just on time he boarded one of the cars and sounded his final whistle as the tram left for the city.'

As a boy, he didn't want for encouragement to play, although he claimed he had no big ambitions: 'Now as a boy and as a youth I never thought I would become a noted footballer. I had my dreams but to me they seemed such wild dreams. I am the only professional footballer in the family. My father followed the game keenly and my brothers William, George, Ewart and Sydney have played but did not aspire to following the game as a profession. In fact, my ambition to make a name as a footballer was a joke in the family circle.'

Perhaps, but not only his immediate family was keen on the game. His cousins played in local church football, while his oldest cousin George was a prominent local sportsman at both football and cricket in the early years of the 20th century. He was a forward and scored regularly for Grimesthorpe Reform Chapel and Grimesthorpe Wesleyans in the Sheffield Free Churches League. As we've seen, both George Barson Snr and Jnr were heavily involved in the Cammell Laird Sports Club.

And then there was Uncle George, his father's brother. George Barson was a keen football follower, to such an extent that he held shares in Sheffield Wednesday, a club he'd watched being established in the 1870s and later

Cammell Laird Sports Pavilion opened

develop into one of the country's finest. What's more, George Barson knew the Clegg brothers, Charles and Colin, who were both prominent amateur athletes in their youth. Charles Clegg would eventually become one of football's greatest administrators and officials. A Sheffield Wednesday director and president, he played for Wednesday and Sheffield FC. (In fact, he was instrumental in the foundation of Sheffield United FC (1889) and was to serve at various times as both chairman and president of the club.) He played for England in the first international with Scotland in 1872, refereed two cup finals in the 1880s and in 1890 he was elected chairman of the FA and FA president in 1923.

Charles Clegg and George Barson shared more than a love of Sheffield Wednesday, however. Both were militant teetotallers and non-smokers, as well as holding fierce religious convictions. It has been said that under Clegg, the Sheffield Wednesday board took a dim view of any player whose drinking or visits to pubs were deemed inappropriate, and there was a pretty restricted view of what was appropriate.

As both president and chairman of the Football League, Charles Clegg would come to spend a considerable amount of time in the coming years mulling over the misbehaviour of George's nephew, Frank. In fact, he would become acquainted with Frank Barson before the latter even signed a full professional form.

Barson's football progress from about 1904 onwards, however, is something of a mystery. The Albion club was for boys and in his memoirs Barson remembers playing for no-one else prior to 1911 when he joined the newly formed Cammell Laird football club.

'I continued to play for the noted Albion but later became a member of the Cammell Laird football team, which was doing well in Sheffield junior circles. Thus, I discarded the zebra-coloured jersey and not without a tinge of regret because my experience with the Albion had been very valuable. My new jersey was far less startling in colour – it was blue. Having earned some notoriety, pleasant and otherwise, as a centre-half I was promptly drafted into that position in my new team. I struck satisfactory form, gaining a regular place in the side.'

Frank was 20 years old when he began playing for the team, and the 1911/12 season would be his one and only taste of Junior League football.

In that inaugural season, Cammell Laird entered the Sheffield-based Hatchard Football League. Founded in 1892, and originally called the Sheffield & District Alliance, it changed its name to the Hatchard Cup League halfway through the 1893/94 season, when local politician Frank Hatchard donated a trophy to the Sheffield & Hallamshire FA.

For many years the cup consisted of numerous divisions, with the top sides from each section proceeding to end-of-season play-offs to determine the overall cup winner. It was predominantly amateur in structure, but professional players were allowed to participate for a season at a time. In their first season, Cammell actually won the Hatchard Cup, defeating local side Hallam before 2,000 spectators at Beighton. Frank, however, would miss the great day for two reasons: First, some months earlier, he'd had his first serious run-in with authority and, second, he'd been simultaneously signed on by Barnsley as a professional. Here he gives his own account of his first serious misdemeanour:

'How I was ordered off for the first time

'We were playing against Dinnington, another local team. The match was fraught with importance. Both teams were well in the running for the local league championship. Soon after the game started, snow began falling heavily. It was often difficult to see the touchline and not easy to distinguish the penalty line. That was how the trouble began.

'Honours were even until late in the second half when the referee awarded a penalty against the Cammell Laird team – I think one of the backs was the offender.

'I do remember distinctly, however, that the foul was not perpetrated inside the penalty box. Although most of the line was covered with snow, a portion was still to be seen and I was in a good position to judge as to the exact locality of the foul. I went to the referee after he had pointed to the penalty spot. "Look here, ref," I

51

shouted, "You have made a mistake. It was outside the penalty area."

"'You go back to your place," replied the referee, "I'm in charge of this game."

'Of course I knew that and I have had good reason to know it since! But I persisted. I was sure my side was being done an injustice. "But ref," I spluttered, "You have made a mistake. You can't give a penalty."

'The official waved me away but I pushed myself in front of him – a very keen but excited young player I can assure you. However, the referee had quite enough of me and he promptly ordered me off the field. It was a big shock when I realised I had to leave the field and yet I considered that I had done the right thing in persisting against the penalty kick.

'But I got a surprise on turning round. My clubmates were following me. They had decided not to remain on the field and so the game was not finished.

'There were a fair number of spectators but I got away all right, although in the opposition camp there was a feeling that I had been responsible entirely for the abrupt stoppage.

'Somehow or other I was not unduly worried about the incident but I knew that I would have to face the music. I went home and did not say anything to my folk about the incident. I guessed that the news would reach the house quickly enough. And it did!

'And some more news came to the house. It was on a postcard addressed to me and summoning me to appear one evening before the local association in connection with the incident already described.'

The Sheffield & Hallamshire FA, who'd ordered Barson to appear before them, was one of J.C. Clegg's many responsibilities, and he personally presided over its disciplinary committees which met at the imposing Wentworth Cafe in the centre of Sheffield. In fact, the committee had to meet twice when dealing with the Barson incident, the first time finding the referee's account wanting. Why, Clegg wanted to know, hadn't Barson been sent off? The second meeting concluded that the Cammell Laird secretary was liable and, along with all the club's players, was severely censured, largely on account of 'presenting unsatisfactory evidence'. The club was fined 10/6d and also had to pay the referee's expenses.

Barson himself recalled his own sentence:

'Severely Cautioned

'I turned up about an hour too soon and I was a very restless youth sitting in the anteroom. Several other miscreants appeared on the scene. They talked of their troubles which really seemed very slight compared to mine. "Frank Barson!"

'I wobbled at the knees when I heard my name called out by one of the officials whom I promptly followed into the room. The gentlemen "on the bench" were not such bad fellows after all. The report of my "offence" was read out and I was asked if I had any explanation to make. The committee listened to me attentively. I was nervous and shaky. I stammered and did not seem able to say half I intended to state. I told the meeting I was keen on the game, keen for my side and felt that I had a right to challenge the decision.

'But it was rightly pointed out to me that the referee was the official in charge of the game and that his word was law and that until I realised that I should find myself in trouble.

'I was conducted out of the room again whilst the meeting deliberated and once more I was in a state of great suspense. It lasted five minutes, although it seemed to be five hours. I was called into the room again.

'"Barson," said one of the committee, "We have decided to caution you – severely. It is your first offence but the next time I am afraid you will be severely punished."

'I thanked the committee – just about as profusely as I would have done if they had been awarding me a medal. I nearly fell over the mat going out, bumped into two smartly dressed young men, who were entering the cafe for their cups of tea, and outside collided with a policeman who nearly mistook me for someone who had not been paying his bill!'

To be fair to Barson, disputes with referees in junior leagues such as the Hatchard's were (and are) fairly common. Hallam, the team Cammell Laird eventually played and beat in the Hatchard Cup Final, had obtained a bye in the semi-final against (coincidentally) the very same Dinnington, a tough outfit from the nearby mining village who'd won the cup for the two previous years running. In a controversial incident, a Dinnington player had kicked a Hallam player and then, like Barson, had refused to go off. The match had been abandoned and awarded to Hallam. Cammell Laird was thus probably lucky to have reached the final and Dinnington might have considered themselves unfortunate.

The fact remained, however, that it had been Frank Barson who'd caused the trouble for Cammell and both his uncle and J.C. Clegg would have been fully aware of his conduct. Barson himself was unmoved, however: 'But after all it did not matter. I escaped lightly but as events turned out I had finished with junior football.'

In fact, while his old team Cammell were winning their one and only trophy, Barson himself was sitting on the trainer's bench as first-team reserve for Barnsley as they won *their* one and only trophy – in the latter's case, the FA Cup.

The approach by Barnsley appeared to have taken Barson by surprise.

'The nature of my work made me very fit and I found that my stamina was a great asset. I played in many hard games never dreaming for a single moment that my exhibitions were being freely discussed in Sheffield football circles and that scouts were being sent by various clubs to keep their eyes upon me. If I had been told so at the time I think that I should have imagined that my leg was being pulled because I really thought that I was a very ordinary junior.'

'That part of Sheffield in which I was reared [was] has been a great hunting ground for Birmingham FC. One of their greatest captures was Frank Womack. The St Andrews club sent a rep to watch me. He was a player – a centre-half. In later years I was told that the Birmingham club made a mistake in sending a centre-half to watch a centre-half – otherwise I might have been sought by Birmingham to whom their representative apparently did not report upon me very favourably.'

When he was approached, it was a very a casual encounter: he was walking one evening in the city just a week after his appearance at the Wentworth Cafe when Arnold Oxspring, a veteran Barnsley half-back who lived in nearby Ecclesfield, stopped him and said, 'Frank, how would you like to play a trial for Barnsley?'

'For a few moments I was sure that he was joking but he soon made it clear to me that the matter was serious.

'"Well," I replied, "I wish I could get the chance though I am not at all sure that I am good enough."

'"But you will come, Frank?" said Oxspring.

'And so I stood on the threshold of a professional career.'

Events then moved swiftly. His instructions were to turn up at Oakwell, Barnsley's ground, just three days after he'd received the invitation from Oxspring, to take part in a reserve match against Castleford. 'And so on the red-letter Thursday in my life I took the train from Sheffield to Barnsley. My cousin, who was keenly interested in my juvenile football career, accompanied me. I became very nervous when I approached the ground.'

Once inside, he was ushered into the dressing room where he changed alongside other debutantes. Out in the ground itself there was a small crowd, many of whom, unbeknownst to Frank, were scouts and club representatives looking out for raw talent. The football grapevine appeared to have been working overtime and Barson was the focus of attention.

'The first kick of the ball I had seemed to give me confidence. I told myself that I must play just as I had played on the recreation grounds around Sheffield and so I did neither more nor less. My work at centre-half

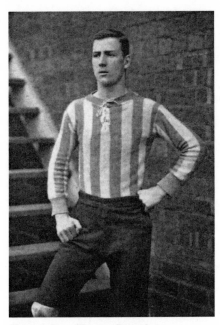

Barson's hero, Tommy Crawshaw

– I was put into that berth without question – came to me quite easily and my feelings can be imagined when I realised that my heading of the ball was evoking applause. I was not optimistic. I did my best.'

Barnsley won 4-1, and Barson had a hand in two of the goals. As he emerged from the team baths his waiting cousin George revealed that there had been a dozen or more managers in the stand and that 'You have been the talk of the match.'

Before he could digest the information, the Barnsley manager Arthur Fairclough appeared. 'Don't hurry away,' he told Barson. 'I want to see you when you are dressed. I want you to become a Barnsley player. Other people are on your track and I want you.'

According to Barson, Barnsley – having paid his fare to the game – were keen not to let him slip away(!). 'I never imagined for a moment that many critical eyes were upon me, that many clubs were represented at Oakwell, that there was going to be a rush for my services and that Barnsley were to make special precautions to ensure that no other club would secure me.'

They adjourned to a nearby hotel, cousin George now close at hand, where Barson was offered 30s a week, a good wage for a reserve in those days. Would he sign that evening?

'I'll sign this minute,' Barson replied, and did so. It was probably the first and only time when he accepted what he was offered without demur. It was largely out of gratitude.

Barson was now anxious to get back to Sheffield. 'I had ceased to be a blacksmith and was now a professional footballer,' he kept repeating to himself. He hurried to the station, knocking people over in his haste. He claimed that while waiting for the train he was approached by scouts from First Division clubs but he was unmoved and unrepentant. 'In junior circles I thought I was not good enough but now Barnsley had singled me out. That was good enough for me. What a great moment in my life!'

At Sheffield, having talked so much his cousin had moved off to another seat, he took the tramcar to Grimesthorpe where he burst into the family home declaring 'I'm a pro!'.

'At first there was a laugh round the family circle. They thought I was joking ("I'm a Pro" being the catchphrase of a famous Music Hall comic character called Stiffy the Goalkeeper played by Harry Weldon) but I very soon convinced them that there was no laugh about the business. My mother knew I was anxious to take up the game seriously. She was delighted on hearing about my successful trial and I may say she never ceased taking a deep interest in my career.

'I finished my week's work at Cammell Lairds where my uncle was engaged, a relative who was also delighted to hear that I had pleased the Barnsley people. He always prophesised that I should make my name in the game and that my appearance in first-class football was only a matter of time.

'It was a happy supper party at the Barson home. Congratulations came from brothers and sisters, neighbours and friends; in fact, if I had been signed on for the biggest club in the country I could not have felt more important.

'At the works I was freely congratulated. The members of the Cammell Laird football team wished me the best of luck ...

'Thus my career opened – and Barnsley paid £5 for me. Not a bad speculation, I think, either for Barnsley or myself!'

All quotations from Barson's autobiography in *Thomson's Weekly News*, May 1925

Chapter Five

Battling Barnsley

*'Pocket money was sparse but occasionally I
used to scrape a few coppers together in order to
visit Hillsborough ... although the prospect of
becoming a Sheffield Wednesday or Sheffield
United player never entered my head.'* **Mems.**

*'They used to say that [Bill Norman] was
never really satisfied unless you had a few
stud marks on our chests. No, I don't mean
he encouraged rough play exactly, but if you
were hurt you hadn't to whimper, if you had
come off ... well, he expected you to be on a
stretcher case and nothing less.'* **Frank Barson
in the *Daily Gazette for Middlesbrough*,
16 November 1939.**

BARSON'S FOOTBALL education would be provided
by the Barnsley club and the half dozen or so top-class

members of the squad who'd watched him at his trial game, men such as Dickie Downs, Bob Glendenning, Phil Bratley, Harry Tufnell, George Lillycrop and Wilf Bartrop. His football inspiration, however, had been provided by the Sheffield Wednesday side of the first years of the 20th century, the team he supported as a youth.

'But how I do remember hurrying off to the Wednesday ground clutching three pennies in my hand and taking up a good post near the rails on the popular side an hour and a half before kick-off. I used to walk five miles there and five miles back, but it was worth it.'[1]

It was a period when Wednesday were experiencing a golden era, and Frank was present during some of their greatest moments: when they lifted the FA Cup twice and won their first Football League title. Whether he sang along to the popular terrace song, adapted from a popular music hall pantomime, is not known.

> 'Play up, Wednesday Boys
> For you'll win whene'er you can,
> And we wish you all good luck,
> For you'll bring us home the cup,
> So play up, old Wednesday Boys'

It must have been a rare occurrence for him to watch the Wednesday in person, however, as admission to Football League matches during this period was not cheap; in fact, at 6d a time, it was relatively expensive. It usually cost only 3d to visit the musical hall, while skilled tradesmen usually received less than £2 a week. There was a purpose behind this prohibitive entrance fee:

> In terms of social class, crowds at Football League matches were predominantly drawn from the skilled working and lower-middle classes ... Social groups below that level were largely excluded by the admission price. The Football League, quite possibly in a deliberate attempt to limit the access of poorer (and this supposedly 'rowdier') supporters, raised the minimum adult male admission price to 6d.[2]

As a junior, Frank Barson was charged 3d, of course, yet it was still a hefty chunk of his 5s 7d a week. However, he was not simply a fan. He was a devotee ...

'My first visit [to Owlerton] provided me with an inspiration. I saw that famous Wednesday player T.H. Crawshaw and that afternoon I decided that I would endeavour to become a centre-half. The Wednesday pivot's play thrilled me. From that day Crawshaw, who was capped against Scotland, Wales and Ireland, became my idol.'[3]

Crawshaw would play for Wednesday between the years 1894 and 1908, racking up 418 appearances in all, and he was the only Sheffield Wednesday player to win two FA Cup winner's medals with the club. In fact, he was just the latest in a line of great Sheffield-born football stars to thrill the city's avid fans. There was William Mosforth, the 'Little Wonder' or 'The Sheffield Dodger' due to his small stature; John

Hunter, a butcher and silver cutler in the city, born in 1852, who won the FA Cup playing at half-back with Blackburn Olympic in 1883 and made seven appearances for England between 1878 and 1882; and the 'Old Warhorse' Billy Betts, a strong, fearless player (with a reputation for being quick-tempered) who played in Wednesday's first FA Cup Final, their first game against Sheffield United, and their first-ever Football League match. Crawshaw had superseded Betts in Wednesday's ranks in 1895.

Raised in the Park Hill area of the town along with his brothers Percy and George, Crawshaw's early football was played with local clubs Park Grange and Attercliffe. He was signed for Wednesday on 24 April 1894, the 1896 publication *Famous Footballers* describing him as, 'A thorough worker always ... he plays a good game from first to last and is unselfish to a degree. A good tackler he uses his head cleverly as well.'[14]

A natural leader, strong-willed, never lacking courage or determination, he led by example and it was said that nobody else fought harder when the chips were down. 'As long as the ball is rolling you can bet we have a chance, and we shall keep going right to the end.' Echoes of things to come.

Barson professed to having been instantly captivated:

'The game had been in progress just a couple of minutes when my attention was riveted on Crawshaw. He headed the ball to perfection, he tackled with power and he slung the ball about with perfect accuracy.

'All the time this thought was running through my mind: "I wish I could do that" and finally I began to jump and kick with such enthusiasm that a gentleman behind me with an upturned clay pipe in his mouth, a voice like thunder and a fist like a mallet settled my excitement for the second half.

'After the game I lingered around the dressing room door in the hope of catching a glimpse of Crawshaw. There were no autograph books in those days. How I would have prized Crawshaw's signature that day or on many days afterwards, but I never saw Crawshaw off the field.

'I did not reveal my secret ambition to my friends. They would have laughed but whenever I got the chance I used to attend the Wednesday matches. My objective was to watch Crawshaw. *No other player interested me.*'[5]

Barson would have been in his teens when he watched Crawshaw perform. He was over 20 years old when he signed for Barnsley but his loyalty to Tommy Crawshaw would never wane. With Barnsley, however, he was confronted with rather more down-to-earth models, men who would shape his outlook on the field of play and a club whose spirit would infuse Barson for the rest of his playing days. Crawshaw might have provided him with his incentive, but Barnsley equipped the fatherless young man with an identity.

In an odd way, Barson's early apprenticeship days at Barnsley mirrored his youthful fan experiences on the Wednesday terraces, but instead of watching from afar as Tommy Crawshaw led his classic team to victory and national acclaim, he now witnessed it at close-hand as Barnsley captain and centre-half Tommy Boyle led his rough-and-ready Second Division outfit as it rampaged into the FA Cup history books. There was a crucial difference, however: Barson was now a participant.

'My interest in my club was soon at fever pitch because as the ties progressed and Barnsley's colours kept flying I felt that I was a real live member of the red brigade, inasmuch as I was regarded as Bratley's understudy and first-reserve half-back in the cup team.'[6]

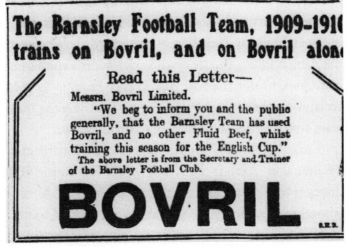

Bovril ad for Barnsley

Two seasons prior to Barson signing for them in 1910, Barnsley had enjoyed a spectacular FA Cup run, beating Blackpool, Bristol Rovers, West Bromwich Albion and Everton to reach the final itself ,where they met Newcastle United. Barnsley led 1-0 until the final minute when Newcastle equalised, Barnsley losing the replay 2-0. The following season they finished 19th in the Second Division and had to apply for re-election.

In 1912, however, just as Barson joined them, they once again began to fight their way to another cup final, defeating along the way Birmingham City, Leicester Fosse, Bolton Wanderers, the holders Bradford City and finally Swindon Town in the semi-final.

In the final itself, in Sheffield, after a drawn first match, they overcame West Bromwich Albion in dramatic fashion. With the score sheet blank at the end of normal time and with just two minutes left of extra time, Glendenning, the Barnsley right-half, beat two opponents and passed ahead to Tuffnell, Barnsley's inside-right. Away Tufnell went on a long dribble through the Albion ranks, finally evading defenders Pennington and Cook to slot the ball past keeper Pearson to wild acclaim. By their victory, Barnsley became only the third team from the Second Division to lift the Cup.

This legendary outfit had been constructed by manager Arthur Fairclough, one of those now disregarded, forgotten characters in football history whose achievements would rank with any of today's acclaimed figures. The team he put together was a mixture of journeymen, raw talent and local youths alongside notables such as Tommy Boyle, George Utley and Glendenning, who would ultimately progress to captain First Division sides. Shortly after achieving his FA Cup triumph, Fairclough left for Huddersfield Town, and over the next seven years he built another successful side despite financial troubles, gaining promotion to the First Division in 1920 and laying the foundations for Herbert Chapman's triple title-winning Terriers side from 1923 to 1926.

Barnsley succeeded in large part because of the tremendous stamina they possessed, sustained throughout the competition. Their fourth-round tie with Bradford City, for example, was a four-game marathon lasting seven hours. They also boasted a superb defence that would concede just four goals in 12 FA Cup matches.

It has been suggested, however, that they were an excessively hard, maybe even unscrupulous, side, and that the team made coordinated attempts to hurt star opponents. The 1912 FA Cup semi-final tie with Southern League Swindon was considered to have been notoriously brutal, with Barnsley setting out to deliberately 'curb the pace' of Swindon's star player, the amateur international Harold Fleming. Barnsley were accused of deliberately kicking Fleming until he was seriously injured.[7] After a 0-0 draw, with Swindon finishing with nine men, Barnsley won the replay 1-0 against a Fleming-less Swindon. In fact, contemporary reports suggest that Fleming entered the first match carrying an injury and departed after some heavy tackles, nothing more sinister than that.

Barnsley's club historian inevitably saw things differently: '[Barnsley] played a hard, uncompromising brand of football that drew comments from quarters that they were a dirty team. The truth was that they were a physical unit that could play football but they possessed a level of fitness that would enable them to *grind out* results. This ability to fight and *wear down* opponents was noted by the press, who christened the club "Battling Barnsley".'[8]

It was also an early manifestation of a modern-sounding counter-attacking policy. The Barnsley captain Tommy Boyle explained in 1914 to readers of the *Sheffield Telegraph Sports Special* that they reinforced an already strong defence by bringing one or both of the inside-forwards back. 'By this method,' he said, 'we often tired the other fellows out; they became somewhat disheartened because their attack yielded nothing tangible and the minute they relaxed their efforts was our opportunity. Then we would set our forwards going, and try to get a goal or two out of our tired opponents.'[9]

In 1913 George Utley, a key Barnsley player at that time, explained that Barnsley were no mere kick and rush team:

> It was not by thoughtless football that Barnsley gained their successes. Many a time – and invariably before a match with a big team – we debated our tactics at length in the dressing room and elsewhere and settled on certain lines of action. Once when we were at Lytham preparing for the cup final, we had begun to talk in this way after dinner. Up jumped the trainer. He collected 22 lumps of sugar and set them all out on the table in the positions of a couple of football 11s and with moves this way and that proceeded to show us how [George] Lillycrop would score the first goal and how we should win 2-0.[10]

Barnsley, for all they were seen as exemplars of the traditional English style, could also modify their approach according to the opposition. When they went to Glasgow to play Celtic in a friendly in 1912, the game finished 1-1, leading the Referee's Notebook column in the *Scottish Umpire* to reflect that, 'We have been accustomed in the past to marvel at the machine-like passing of Aston Villa, and the brilliant individualism of some of the West Bromwich players, but never before have we seen just such a combination of artistic ability, unbounded enthusiasm and dare-devil tactics as that furnished by the Yorkshiremen. Some people seemed not to like the dare-devil part of the game, but it is the new English style.'[11]

FRANK BARSON

Barson himself had no doubts about their abilities:

'I have often been asked whether they were really good footballers. My reply is always a very emphatic "yes". Those men did not trouble about the frills, but played good straight-from-the-shoulder football. They were all good enough to attract the biggest clubs in the country. Was I not fortunate, then, in being "drilled" amongst these great players?'[12]

Barson would also be 'drilled' by a man who was as instrumental in creating the Barnsley side as Fairclough himself – the Oakwell trainer, Bill Norman. A devotee of 'physical culture', Norman was an old soldier in more senses than one, being an ex-drill sergeant in the army, as well as an accomplished gymnastics instructor. After serving at Aldershot, Malta, Cairo and Cape Town, he finished his army days instructing the cadets at Sandhurst before moving into football full time.

Norman would leave Barnsley in 1913 to follow Arthur Fairclough to Huddersfield Town, but his approach and technique were surprisingly modern if one is to believe that legendary football writer and critic Tityrus (aka Jimmy Catton).

> Norman is more than a trainer. I know a youngster in the B team – Moore to wit – who could give Norman a testimonial. Since Moore has come under this mentor he has increased 8lb in weight and five or six yards in speed. But Norman is more than a physical culture man. He talks football to his men, he impresses on them *that the ball must be their first objective and he discusses tactics.* He is a firm believer in the half-backs playing close up to the opposing forwards and giving them little time in which to work.[13]

Norman will reappear in Barson's story some years later. For now, however, he was a key factor in Barson's apprenticeship as the latter moved steadily through the ranks, his promotions occurring as bigger clubs came in to lure away Barnsley's heroes. The dismantling of the FA Cup team was rapid.

In September 1911 team captain Tommy Boyle left for Burnley for £1,250. In close season 1912 manager Fairclough departed, and in March 1913 centre-back Glendenning went to Bolton Wanderers for £1,200, soon to be followed by top-scorer George Lillycrop in August that year for £1,300, also to Bolton. In November 1913 left-half George Utley went to Sheffield United for £2,000. Others followed but the departures of Glendenning and Utley from the half-back line were significant for Barson, who by season 1913/14 had become a regular first-team player, first at right-half and then centre-back.

'Phil Bratley was playing wonderful football. He had succeeded Tommy Boyle who had gone to Burnley, and the Barnsley directors decided to rest him for some of the league games. My first game as a member of the first team was against Leicester Fosse and my display was considered very satisfactory.'[14]

By the summer of 1914 yet more Barnsley cup heroes had departed, including Barson's mentor, Phil Bratley, and star forward Wilf Bartrop. The glory days were well and truly over, but there was one important member of the 1912 cup team who had chosen to remain, despite overtures from First Division clubs – full-back Dickie Downs.

'BC', writing in the *Green 'Un* on 31 January 1914, dubbed Downs 'Barnsley's Bulwark'. Two years earlier, Jimmy Catton had waxed lyrical:

> Downs is not the weight of Crompton. He has not the height and the long legs of McCracken but he is parcel of pluck, his judgement atones for his medium stature and his foot generally reaches the right part of the ball at precisely the exact time. Downs is 24, comes out under the standard

of 5ft 6.5 inches and brings the beam down at 12 stones. A solid man, he has a tendency to bowed legs, which are like pillars to support him. These players who have a bow in the legs are generally sturdy and skilful. Why is it? Is it because this formation renders more support to the body? But Downs has a chest – a heart inside it. I cannot imagine his heart ever flutters. Dark hair, sallow skin, and steady, fixing riveting eyes, with a firm-set mouth convince all and sundry that he takes his football as seriously as any workman his wages.[15]

Downs would be the first Barnsley player to obtain national recognition, being selected as early as 1910 for a Football League 11; he was an ever-present in the Barnsley side from his introduction in 1908 until he left to join Everton in 1920; he eventually overtook Albert Oxspring's club appearance record to become the first Barnsley player to make over 300 appearances.

He was also a firm Players' Union man and recruited Frank Barson to serve as club representative. The two of them attended Players' Union meetings in Manchester, on one occasion helping to fight off a League attempt to abolish player bonuses. Downs was also an organiser for the Players' Union sports days, taking along a Barnsley team that in 1912 won the tug-of war (of course), the half-mile relay race and even – in the person of 'Bill' Norman – second place in the 60 yards trainers' race.

Tityrus considered Downs an exemplary tackler: 'The three points in his football which appeal to me are: his ability to be in the right position, his precise timing of the ball let it come as it will, and his honest tackling. His tackling is robust but he does not make the man his first consideration. Beyond all manner of doubt his first objective is the ball. Possibly he may take both – but he rarely misses the ball.'[16]

Charles Buchan, writing many years later, felt otherwise. Downs was one of the first defenders to employ the sliding tackle: 'In my opinion, this tackle which I first saw introduced by Dicky Downs ... has done more than anything else, except the change in the offside law in 1925, to alter the character of the game.' Although completely legal, Buchan felt that the tackle 'increased the pace at which the game was played and the amount of physical contact.'[17]

Whatever Buchan felt, Downs's style suited the emerging force called Frank Barson. The two men formed a formidable partnership: Downs's overhead kicks and on-line clearances, his great powers of recovery and tremendous volleying of the ball, combined with Barson's fearless heading, distribution and powerful surges upfield; together they helped Barnsley consolidate in the final two years before the First World War years, so much so that the club ended the 1914/15 season in their highest league position ever – third place.

Indeed, so successful a partnership were they that in November 1912 it was reported that an unnamed club had made a £2,500 offer for the pair of them. Barnsley turned it down ('We are not prepared to transfer any of our players at any price'). It was also commented at the time: 'They have high hopes of Barson. He is said to be of more promise than Boyle ever was and so they hope to realise top quotations for him.'[18]

There was, however, one aspect of Downs's play that was in stark contrast to his junior partner. Jimmy Catton observed:

> Downs is not the man who 'spreads dismay around' by converting himself into a battering ram or by rushes akin to the infuriated bull. A sane, cool, skilful, clean and fair player ...[19]

For Barson, however, he had found his football university:

'All the Barnsley Cup heroes were good to me. Most of them called a spade a spade. They didn't hesitate to criticise my weaknesses on the field. At different times one or the other would talk to me. Their criticism was helpful. Individualism was a minor quality at Barnsley – team-work was demanded. I pleased the Barnsley folk. It was declared that I showed signs of developing into a player after their own heart. They said that with more experience I should soon be serving up the stuff wanted at Oakwell – good, old-fashioned football, the fearless shoulder charge, the strong heading of the ball, the lusty distributive work and the never-say-die defensive tactics. Well I tried to play along those lines.'

He added, however: 'I had never forgotten Crawshaw of the Wednesday. Whenever I played in those early days I fashioned my style after him.'[20]

Endnotes

1. Mems
2. Dave Russell, *Football and the English: A Social History of Association Football in England*, (Carnegie, 1997)
3. Mems
4. Charles Alcock (ed), *Famous Footballers and Athletes* (London: Huson, 1896-97)
5. Mems
6. Mems
7. wmpickford.blogspot.com, Frank Barson : the finest football brain of his time, 19 August 2007
8. Grenville Firth, *Oakwell – The Official History of Barnsley FC*, 2012
9. *Sheffield Telegraph Sports Special*, 1914
10. Jonathan Wilson, *Inverting the Pyramid* (London: Orion, 2008), p.29
11. Quoted in Jonathan Wilson, *Inverting the Pyramid* (London: Orion, 2008), p.32
12. Mems
13. *Athletic News*, 8 April 1912
14. Mems
15. *Athletic News* 8 April 1912
16. Ditto
17. Charles Buchan, *A Lifetime In Football* (The Sportsman's Book Club, 1956), p.71
18. *Dundee Courier*, 30 November 1912
19. *Athletic News*, 8 April 1912
20. Mems

Chapter Six

Barson's Bombshell

*'As in my junior days, my enthusiasm at
Barnsley quickly led to my coming under
the notice of referees to say nothing of the
spectators at different grounds. To put it
broadly, I "got my name up". I think my tall
stature, making me rather conspicuous, and
the persistent efforts I made to head the ball
were greatly responsible …'* **Mems.**

IT WOULD take Barson two seasons of understudying
before he became a regular first-team player for Barnsley.
In early 1912 he first appears for them in the Midland
League but by August 1912 he is taking part in trial
games, playing for the reserves in the Central League and
eventually he replaces second-team centre-half Hanlon,
who is returned to Darlington whence he came. In
December 1912 Barson replaces Tom Utley in another
trial game and by the end of season 1912/13 he is the

regular first-team reserve, having made five first-team appearances.

He would start the 1913/14 season at right-half and make 38 appearances, helping Barnsley to fifth place in Division Two. The following season he would move to centre-half and make 34 appearances, and Barnsley did even better, finishing in third place, three points off promotion.

He was then 25 years old but these would be the only two regular seasons he would complete with Barnsley. The First World War meant the end of professional football for four years and by the time it finished Barson would be 28. His experience as a footballer thus paled into insignificance when compared to his work as a blacksmith, the job he first commenced when aged 12 and which he only finally left in 1919.

Not surprisingly, perhaps, he tended to ascribe much of his legendary stamina to his work in the steelworks rather than to the military-style training imposed by 'Sergeant Major' Norman.

Barson did claim to have been influenced by a number of key players in his early days, but the curious thing is, none of them displayed the outright aggressions and venom that would come to characterise Barson's game as he rose through the ranks. Bratley, Boyle, Downs, Utley, Taylor, Glendenning – all were clearly tough and hard-working players, but none would suffer the disciplinary problems that would beset Barson. His idol, Tommy Crawshaw, was also equally blemish-free.

At times it would seem that he was taking the world onto his shoulders, seeking out injustice and perfidy where in fact none existed. His uncontrolled temper would wreak damage mainly to himself. As the esteemed football writer Ivan Sharpe commented, 'He is a good case for those who study psychology.'[1]

In the early years of his professional career, however, much of the trouble to come seemed a distant prospect, although there were occasional signs that his antipathy towards the refereeing fraternity would become a major problem.

In January 1914 Barnsley met First Division Liverpool in the first round of the FA Cup and by all accounts were unlucky to lose 1-0 in a replay. Barson himself played poorly but one person who did shine in the match was the referee, Herbert Bamlett.

Bamlett was one of the first 'personality' referees, those men in black who develop a distinctive style and technique that make them stand out and be noticed. Bamlett would become the youngest referee to officiate in an FA Cup Final that very year, although the football writer 'BC' for the *Green 'Un* considered his methods highly unusual, even controversial:

THE LIGHTNING REFEREE

You see, the great thing about Bamlett is that he is quick, very. You know the kind of referee who hears a shout of 'foul', has a slight idea himself that there has been one, and then, just as the crowd seems about to lynch him, he blows. Well, Bamlett is the other way round; he sees fouls and gives them before an excited partisan would guess that anything has happened.[2]

This ability of Bamlett's was unique, but 'not an unmixed virtue,' however:

I really believe that Bamlett has got second sight, for many times I have watched him prepare for a foul which up to then had no existence save in the mind of the man about to break the law.

Bamlett has seen that, has blown for the foul 'about to be' and then there has been no foul which has made Bamlett look foolish, for after all to break the law of football in thought is not an indictable offence.[3]

Liverpool Echo football columnist 'Bee' was full of admiration for him, however:

> The game was like the referee – hard. Play was fast, it was clever, dogged, and the pace did not slacken. It was a great game – keen, clean with one exception [when Travers kicked Pursell and the fighting pose was adopted by both players]. Referee Bamlett was unable to see the offence referred to but he was very emphatic in informing the players that he would stand no nonsense, and that any further offence would mean that the player concerned would be ordered from the field. His control of the game was capital, and it was his determined stoppage of the first rough incident that ensured [rough spoiling] tactics being impossible.[4]

Bamlett had already made his presence felt earlier in the year, however, at Barson's home ground of Oakwell where he had shocked the home supporters by apparently reporting their cat-calling and loud criticisms to the football authorities. It was clear that Bamlett felt that the conduct of some Barnsley supporters had become so disorderly as to seriously threaten the pursuit of the game.

According to the *Sheffield Daily Telegraph*, however, the incident was 'Much Ado About Nothing':

All that transpired was a temporary stoppage of the game by Mr Bamlett the referee, who took exception to certain remarks made by a few members of the crowd behind the Huddersfield goal after he had disallowed a point scored by Travers on the ground of offside. The referee complained to Mr Hastie the club secretary who went to the fringe of the crowd and the game continued without more than a few of the 8,000 spectators knowing what had occurred.[5]

The paper accused some reporters of spreading 'false news': 'The magnifying of a "molehill into a mountain" and the "mud-flinging" inference therein contained is calculated to bring odium on the club. It is quite certain that such exaggeration will have aroused the indignation of all of Barnsley's spectators who have the interest of the club at heart.'[6] There was certainly indignation, and when the Lightning Referee reappeared at Oakwell in February to referee a match between Barnsley and Grimsby Town, he was struck by something rather less electric. The *Green 'Un* reported:

SERIOUS ACCIDENT TO REFEREE BAMLETT. REFEREE KNOCKED OUT

One portion of the game seemed a veritable chapter of accidents. Martin came in contact with Barson and had to leave the field for a time while a moment later an unusual incident occurred in which Barson again figured. The referee, Mr H.S. Bamlett of Gateshead, collided heavily with Barson giving his head a hard bang. But it was soon evident that the matter was of a somewhat serious nature. Mr Bamlett was picked up but it was some time before he came properly round. He then had to go off and one of the linesmen, Mr T.S. Sephton of Derby, took charge of the game. It transpired that Mr Bamlett had sustained a slight concussion and had rather a severe cut on the face. A quarter of an hour after the interval he reappeared with his face patched and, amid loud applause, resumed control of the game.[7]

Frank Barson recalled the incident as follows:

'I came under the warning note of a couple of referees and on one occasion at Barnsley when we were playing Grimsby Town I bumped into one of those officials in a most unceremonious manner. It was an accident but today that referee still remembers the incident. In this game I was pitching into it with great vigour. I remember slinging out the ball to our left-winger with a robust charge and then I recall the referee shouting to me to "go steady". I went on, he followed, and then I turned suddenly, I collided with him and the official was laid out. It was, as I have said, an accident and I was very sorry about it. Mr Bamlett got a nasty knock but he soon resumed.'[8]

The *Week and Sports Special* reporter noted, 'The spectacle of a referee in difficulties seems invariably to tickle a crowd and there was much laughter when Mr Bamlett went down but it was soon turned to sympathy when he was carried off, evidently badly hurt.'[9]

Now whether or not the 'Barnsley Bump' administered to Bamlett was an accident or not, we shall never know, although it's unlikely. Nonetheless, Bamlett was somewhat accident-prone. A few years prior to this a blow from a football had loosened his teeth in a game at Bristol, while at Goodison Park in 1910 a shot from forward Sharp had knocked him over.

Mr. H. S. BAMLETT,
League Referee.

It would not be the end of the affair for Barson, however. The linesman, T.S. Sephton, who took up the flag from Bamlett when the latter was KO'd, would soon reappear in Barson's life, and exact retrospective revenge. (Bamlett would also return – to became Barson's manager at Manchester United!)

The following season, Barson moved to centre-half, as Phil Bratley left the club. Barson struggled at first: during a 7-0 defeat at the start of the season it was commented,

> No one can dispute Barson's unflagging energy but something more than speed and honest plugging is required for a position which can be described as the 'centre of gravity'.

> Barson worked tremendously hard at Derby
> but much of his energy was wasted and until he
> ripens in intuition and learns the greater value of
> keeping the ball low he will not make a mainspring
> calculated to set the team smoothly going.[10]

He would recover, however, and was soon the centrepiece of a solid and reasonably successful Barnsley side. In the FA Cup, though, those old Barnsley traditions were not enough to prevent another first-round exit, once again to a team from Merseyside, although it cannot be said that Barson went down without a fight.

In fact, the Everton–Barnsley FA Cup tie would hit the headlines: 'The Everton Sensations' (*Athletic News*); 'Sensational Cup Ties' (*Liverpool Echo*); 'Remarkable Tie' (*Leeds Mercury*) (although the *Yorkshire Evening Post* summed up the events as 'Players Silly Quarrel on the Field'). It would also be the moment when the refereeing fraternity hit back.

The *Liverpool Echo* reporter had no doubts as to who caused the initial disturbance:

> Barson started the rumpus that made the game
> stand before the football world as a disgrace. His
> foul on Clennell was meant and was severe. He
> was cautioned. Then Barson and Harrison got to
> loggerheads and a linesman wisely pointed out
> something that the strict referee had not seen.
> Referee Sephton thereupon spoke to the two players.
>
> Then the tragedy tinged with comic effects.
> Barson whipped the feet from under Harrison who

retaliated by allegedly kicking Barson. The sight of the injured Barnsley man being attended to by his trainer and the players in clusters talking heatedly was clinched when [both were sent off and] the two men walked towards the players' subway. Nearing this subway the players shook hands – what for is hard to understand.[11]

Later in the game, another Everton player, Parker, was dismissed for kicking at the Barnsley keeper, and when two more Everton players left the field due to illness the Toffees ended the game with just seven men on the pitch. Nevertheless, Everton still ran out winners 3-0.

The on-field shenanigans caused trouble on the terraces, however. At the end, referee Sephton had to be 'cloaked' as he left the field by Liverpool secretary Cuff and several players while incidents of 'fruit-throwing' had already occurred. After the game, a crowd gathered outside Goodison and had to be dispersed by the police. The referee and a linesman were then spirited away in a taxi.

The trouble was laid clearly at Barnsley's feet: 'Barnsley are noted cup fighters and it is also well known that the Yorkshire team forsake the scientific for the more robust and vigorous methods.' The reporter added, that the 'reprehensible tactics' of certain players was considered to have ruined the game as a contest.[12]

The player in question remembered it all quite differently.

'I quite admit that I played a very vigorous game that afternoon. I was putting some of the real Barnsley zest into the struggle. That afternoon a young fellow George Harrison – now with Preston North End – was scintillating on the Everton left wing. I have a great admiration for Harrison, a very sportsman-like player.

'At this time he was on the threshold of his career and he was very keen, and rightly so, and so was I. I went for him for all I was worth, and George, rightly so, handed out the stuff I deserved but neither of us was of the opinion that we had overstepped the mark, although the crowd was on my track. Finally the referee cautioned the pair of us. The struggle went on.

'Everton were enjoying undoubted superiority. Harrison suddenly went off at top pace. It was a brilliant run. I went after him. I tried to tackle him but missed. The tackle was adjudged to be illegal. Harrison had just centred the ball when I made a dive at him. In the excitement of the moment Harrison made a movement towards me which I did not mind but which the referee disliked to say nothing of what he thought of my attempted tackle. And the crowd they hooted at me.

'The referee agreed with them and sent me off. He also sent off Harrison. Who was to blame? Why Barson! they said. Barson, of course. He should have been sent off before.

'It is an old story now but I do not think that I deserved marching orders. After all, it was a cup tie and cup ties are tense struggles – always! But there was something else I was certain about and that was Harrison's misfortune. In my opinion he did not merit this treatment. Both of us stood for a few moments as if hypnotised. The crowd continued to shout. Players on both sides appealed to the referee but that official refused to reconsider his decision.

'And then there was a dramatic incident. Harrison and myself, just before we commenced to leave the field, stopped to shake hands. It was a spontaneous action. Harrison realised he had my sympathy and likewise I knew that the Everton man was sorry I was involved.

'The crowd appeared to alter their views a little. They were sure Harrison was not to blame and possibly they were beginning to think that I was not such a miscreant after all. And so we disappeared into our dressing rooms. What happened to the delinquents? Well, we dressed and went into the stand to watch the finish of the game. We sat near one another. No one appeared to notice us.'

After the match, however, Barson appeared to feel that the crowd outside were looking for him, not referee Sephton:

'Our officials deemed it advisable that I should not leave the ground with the rest of the players. I might be singled out by some of the crowd. So I slipped out at another door, hurried along to a waiting taxi, in which two of our officials were seated, and buzzed off to the Central Station. When the other members of the team were coming out each face was rather keenly scanned by a waiting crowd. But Barson had flown!'[13]

* * *

With the outbreak of the First World War, Barson's home town of Sheffield was rapidly transformed into the armaments citadel of the Empire. As Lloyd George, the Minister of Munitions, recognised in November

1915, 'this is a war of material above everything else', and the Steel City of Sheffield made a vital contribution to the industrial battlefield. 'This is ... an engineer's war – everything depends upon rapid and efficient production of fighting material in vast quantities, and we are, therefore, face to face with the necessity of a dual army, one in the field, the other in the production of munitions.'[14]

In the Sheffield region at the beginning of the war the five big armament firms (Vickers, John Brown, Hadfield's, Cammell Laird and Thomas Firth) were making no more than 1,000 shells per week, or 52,000 per annum, but by the end of 1917 the region was making approximately six million per annum. For every shell produced in 1914, the area was producing 115 in 1917.

There were significant developments at each Cammell works. The Cyclops factory was provided with new shops and plant for the heat treatment of gun forgings, while the area covered by the projectile shop at Grimesthorpe was increased almost six-fold. When the war began it employed 130; by December 1918 it employed 3,000. The factory turned out armour plate for tanks, grenades, shells, howitzer bomb heads, trench howitzers as well as shrapnel-proof steel helmets. In fact, Grimesthorpe was significant enough to be bombed by Zeppelins.

Barson's life changed dramatically. 'It fell to my lot to be engaged in munitions work in the war period. I worked at my trade in Sheffield and it was very hard work too. I was able to play football for Barnsley but never on any occasion did I lose any time at the workshop. On scores of occasions I have worked day and night – sometimes I have stepped onto the field after nearly 24 hours in the shop and think I can claim a little in helping to keep the Barnsley colours flying.'[15]

Wartime football, although eventually organised into leagues, was no substitute for the real thing. Men were paid to play, sometimes £1 a week, but teams were haphazardly put together. Barson recalled, 'Frequently we were hard up for a team. I have known occasions when we have had four or five players short and I have gone onto the grandstand to canvas for players. We got a lot of volunteers and it was really surprising how well the deputies performed.'[16]

In fact, in the first season Barnsley lost matches heavily, disrupted as they often were by wartime recruitment and the lack of ability of men to travel easily. When war broke out, of 36 players on the books, 22 were in khaki, three were in the mines and one [Barson] on munitions. During a later Barnsley match it was revealed that six of the players worked in coalmines, four in munitions, and one was a soldier on leave.

Barson had another responsibility, however. In October 1915, he married one Frances Evelyn Betton, a miner's daughter from New Tupton in Derbyshire. There was a football connection. New Tupton Ivanhoe was a thriving local side and one of Frances's cousins would later play for Newcastle United.

It's only speculation, but Barson's newly wedded state may well have been the reason why on 18 October he turned up for a match against Leeds City three minutes late, complaining that he couldn't get a taxi. Barnsley lost 7-1 without him and he didn't play again that season.

When he did return, as he put it, 'Although the football was not of the real standard I used to put my heart and soul into every game. I had to go the whole hog and, of course, I paid the penalty.'[17]

In October 1917, in a match against Birmingham, Barson appeared to lose control.

'My recollection of this incident is rather hazy. A few clouds have rolled by since that day! I remember, however, that I was playing at centre-half and during a rather strenuous game I cut across at top speed to meet a very fleet outside-left whose name has completely gone out of my mind. It was my intention to block the ball. To this day I think I blocked it fairly and squarely.

'Unfortunately for me the winger went flying over. There were howls of disapproval and expressions of delight from the crowd when the referee promptly ordered "your humble" to the dressing rooms.

'I thought that I was being harshly dealt with. So did my colleagues. So did our officials but I realised that it would be unwise to challenge the decision.'[18]

The *Sheffield Daily Telegraph* disagreed:

> Barson, however, had only himself to blame. He was looking for trouble all the afternoon and his action was the more inexplicable in that he was the only man on either side who was in an unduly militant mood.
>
> Both Birmingham and Barnsley are fairly hard sides and a few good charges make little or no difference to either. But the writer is bound to say that Barson was deliberately rough on at least three

occasions and he had incurred marked censure before he was given marching orders. Just before the edict went forth he had deliberately charged Womack when that player was to all intents and purposes out of the game.

The writer did feel that there were some mitigating circumstances, however:

BARSON'S MISFORTUNE

There was just one point which made people make a slight excuse for Barson. Just as his temperature was at blood heat Ball kicked him in the stomach. The act was quite unintentional; as a matter of fact, Ball practically had his back to his opponent when he tried to hook the ball but he took poor Barson full in the stomach. Immediately that he got right the Barnsley man rushed across the field, kicked Best's legs from under him as he was going for goal and hurt him rather badly. The referee immediately ordered off Barson and he deserved all that he received. If there had been feeling in the game generally there might have been some excuse but he had all the ill-humour to himself.[19]

The *Birmingham Sports Argus* concluded:

The ordering off of Barson was unfortunate and I am afraid he was made the scapegoat of others' indiscretions. Barson is a big, vigorous player. Prior to this happening he had been no worse than any of the others but unquestionably he went too far when he felled Ernest Best. He seemed to race across the field deliberately to stop him. He stopped him, but by kicking his legs from under him. It was not football. It was not the act of a sportsman but Barson was not the only sinner. There were others who did unfair tricks in a startling way but they were undiscovered.[20]

Despite this being a wartime game, punishment was swift:

'The verdict! Two months suspension. But some people thought that I should not worry because after all we were not receiving wages at this time; we were simply being paid expenses. They were wrong. I was much upset about this punishment. I felt that I had been unfairly punished – very unfairly.

'And what is more, I do not think my opponent who did the spinning-wheel trick really thought I earned this drastic treatment.

'But you get over these things in football ...'[21]

Barson's ill-humour cannot have been helped by the fact that a week or so later he was fined for not paying his fare for a railway journey. He had been travelling on the Grand Central Railway and as he passed through Victoria Station, he'd tendered a platform ticket, was stopped, interrogated and charged. In his defence he claimed that he had journeyed from Penistone, having previously accompanied an injured player there from Barnsley by motorcar. He would appear to have been on club duty, therefore. Although seemingly innocuous, an argument over travel and its accompanying costs would have deep ramifications for Barson's subsequent career.

However, this misdemeanour would not prevent his being presented to the king in 1919 as the latter passed through the Cammell Laird munitions works and visited the workshop where he and his uncle worked.

With the war over, it wasn't long before 'reps' from bigger football clubs such as Everton, Newcastle and Manchester United started appearing at Oakwell, intent on signing Barnsley's star player. Charlie Roberts, having left the Players' Union and taken up the managerial post at Oldham, was particularly keen on him, but Barnsley declared that they would not be selling anyone.

Unfortunately for the club, they had been 'cheated' out of a First Division place that might have inclined Barson to stay where he was. Put simply, for the first season following the war, the First Division had been extended to 22 clubs, thus creating an extra four places. The top two teams in Division Two at the end of season 1914/15 were thus promoted, while relegated Spurs were re-elected.

That left one extra place which by rights should have gone to Barnsley, who'd finished third in Division Two. However, the League decided to hold a ballot for the vacancy and Arsenal, who had finished well below Barnsley in Division Two, secured more votes. Barnsley appealed but to no avail.

Nevertheless, season 1919/20 began amiably enough, with Barson taking his benefit, a match against Rotherham that produced a record £420. (By contrast, Arnold Oxspring, the man who'd scouted him for the club, had received just £64 11s 6d when his benefit match was played in June 1907.)

Barson was grateful: 'A tidy sum it was too. I shall never forget my Barnsley friends. They rallied round that day and I may say that in the colliery town I still prize many of my staunch friendships.'[22] He would soon put them to the test, however. In late September 1919 a national rail strike began. It would last just nine days, but long enough to cause trouble between Barson and the club.

'I was living in Sheffield and travelling to and fro from Barnsley each day ... at the time there were two other Barnsley players living in Sheffield. They were young lads and of course they were not getting the wage I was receiving.

'Well, one day during a railway strike there were no through trains from Sheffield to Barnsley. We were, however, determined to get through to Oakwell in order to do our training, and accordingly travelled some distance on a bus. It is true we had railway contract tickets – fairly expensive items – and it is also quite true that we appreciated the consideration of the club in allowing us to reside out of Barnsley.

'However, I thought it quite reasonable that, on behalf of these young players, I should raise the question of the bus fares to an official of the club in the hope of having the money refunded to the lads. Personally I did not care a jot about my own expenses!

'Well, as the saying goes, I got a bump!'

The official surprised Barson by asking him if he thought the club was 'a charitable institution'. 'No',

Barson replied, he just thought it reasonable that the lads, through no fault of their own, were out of pocket and should get their money back.

'I became annoyed, very annoyed, and did not hesitate to express my annoyance.'

In the ensuing argument Barson admitted he made remarks concerning the club in general that were 'not parliamentary'.

'"You know Frank," the official said, "you would not say such things if a director were present."

'"Yes I would," I replied hotly.'

And lo and behold a director appeared, to which Barson made the same remarks in language, 'not of drawing room order'.[23]

He was asked to apologise but refused and declared that he wanted to go on to the transfer list.

On 17 October, the club issued yet another statement declaring that no one was going to be transferred. A week later, however, beneath a headline declaring 'Barson Bombshell', the *Yorkshire Telegraph* broke the news that Frank Barson had been transferred to Aston Villa.

Barson himself claimed to have been unaware of Villa's interest until the last moment.

'I was carrying on training work in the dressing room when one of the club officials came in and said that I was wanted in the office. I dressed and then learned that at a hotel in Barnsley a stranger was waiting to see the club official and myself.

'"How would you like to go to a First Division club?" asked the official.

'"Great," I said. "Who is it waiting to see us?"

'"Aston Villa," I was informed.

'We walked to the hotel. There sitting before the fire was a gentleman with whom I was destined to become very intimately acquainted. He was Mr George Ramsey, the secretary of Aston Villa.

'"Would you like to join the Villa?" asked Ramsey.

'"Very much so," I replied, "but I am afraid I am not class enough for such a swell team."'[24]

Despite his apparent misgivings, Barson signed. His Barnsley days were over. There was a great deal of regret on behalf of supporters at Barson's sale, and some criticism of the club for actually letting him go. They had offered him the maximum wage and thus could have refused his (three) requests to leave, but the fee offered was large, a record, and had he stayed a season he could well have decamped to the Southern League the following year for nothing.

The *Yorkshire Telegraph* concluded:

But the mischief is done. Barson has gone...[25]

Endnotes

1. *Athletic News,* 21 September 1925
2. *Green 'Un,* 31 January 1914
3. Ditto
4. *Liverpool Echo,* 16 January 1914
5. *Sheffield Daily Telegraph,* 3 January 1914
6. Ditto
7. *Green 'Un,* 7 February 1914
8. Mems
9. *Week and Sports Special,* 14 February 1914
10. *Daily Herald,* 2 September 1914
11. *Liverpool Echo,* 11 January 1914
12. *Lancashire Daily Post,* 11 January 1914
13. Mems
14. *The Engineer,* 28 May 1915, p.553
15. Mems
16. Ditto
17. Ditto
18. Ditto
19. *Sheffield Daily Telegraph,* 1 October 1917
20. *The Birmingham Sports Argus,* October 1917
21. Mems
22. Ditto
23. Ditto
24. Ditto
25. *Yorkshire Telegraph,* 24 October 1919

Chapter Seven

The Barnsley Punch

'Barson, once of Barnsley, now Aston Villa, is the beau ideal of a centre-half for teams that are not crazy about science. "Tophole at cutting 'em down" is how a brother "pro" described him. The Villa started late this season, and a beautiful bit of machinery of pre-war type was not possible. Barson has a roving commission, and delivers the goods.' **Sideline Whispers, *The Globe*, Saturday, 29 November 1919.**

'The Villa boys had heard a lot about me. A few of then chipped me. One said, "Now Frank, you will have to put on your patent leather boots." I knew that the inference was I should be expected by some people to cut out some of my Barnsley vigour. "Nay, lad, I can't drop the Barnsley Punch."' **Mems.**

IN OCTOBER 1919, Frank Barson was briefly Britain's most expensive player. The fee was 'withheld' at first but later revealed to be some £2,850. It was soon eclipsed as football clubs cashed in on the boom in attendances that occurred with the war's end and the sudden need to replenish depleted squads. In the same month the flamboyant centre-forward Jack Cock moved from Huddersfield to Chelsea, boasting in November that his fee was, 'the biggest ever known, and not a penny less than £3,000'. In December, Manchester City paid Preston North End £3,000 for Mick Hamill, while the following year Plymouth Argyle's David Jack would cost Bolton Wanderers £3,500. By 1922 the record had reached the then unheard-of figure of £5,000 paid for Syd Puddefoot by Scottish side Falkirk.

All the same, it was unusual for Aston Villa to pay so much. Some years later Fred Rinder, chairman of Villa, was interviewed by Jimmy Catton and took the opportunity to emphasise that it was a 'one-off':

'On this subject of transfer fees I should like to say that Aston Villa have not been in the habit of going abroad with unlimited cheques and buying players. The history of Aston Villa proves that we have never been financial speculators in football players. Whatever successes we may have had are not due to the use of money, as if it was the talisman to make the team. You may scatter gold over the land, but it does not follow that a good harvest will be gathered in. The fee for Barson is the highest the club has ever paid. No one else has cost us half as much money.'[1]

Barson later revealed that though he cost a lot in transfer fees, his wages were less impressive. Senior

players at the club were receiving the then maximum of £8 while he was on £7 from the start. He claimed that when manager Ramsey called him into the office to sign: 'In those days I was the keen type, thinking only of the football and not the money so I didn't stop even to talk about my wages. "I'm in a bit of a hurry," I said, "So if I sign it can you fill in the details later?" Naturally I assumed I would be on top money but Ramsey merely filled in £7 instead of £8 and I had to stick to that rate all the season.'[2]

Given the later tales of Barson's pecuniary astuteness, it's hard to believe but then he was just slightly overawed at joining such an illustrious club. It was a considerable fee for a defender and there was a definite sense of unease at his sudden expensive elevation. Would he be good enough? Was he stepping out of his comfort zone?

'I am afraid I am not class enough for such a swell team,' he is supposed to have commented to Villa secretary G. H. Ramsey. 'But I will do my best for you.'

'That's the spirit,' Mr Ramsey replied.

At the same time, being Frank Barson, there was a touch of defiance about him. 'I realised I was to figure among more classy players but artistry does not always win matches and lost matches make for long faces in the directors' and managers' rooms.'

There had certainly been some long faces in the Villa director's lounge of late. The opening months of the 1919/20 season had been a disaster for the club. On 18 October, after ten games, they were bottom of the First Division having won just one game and lost eight.

'Was it expected that I was to bring success like magic? I am not a nervous chap, but I quaked a lot when I thought of my first appearance as a Villan.'[3]

The truth was, Barson was joining an institution which, despite its on-field woes, was the closest thing to football royalty. Aston Villa had been one of the dozen teams to compete in the inaugural Football League in 1888. One of the club's directors, William McGregor, was the Football League's founder, the venerable 'Father of Football'.

Villa had been the most successful English club of the Victorian era and by the start of the First World War had won the First Division championship six times and the FA Cup five times. Manager/secretary George

Ramsey had led them to every one of those triumphs and could thus boast a record second only to Sir Alex Ferguson and Arsene Wenger in each competition, respectively.

The roll-call of famous 'Villans', whom Barson was now expected to live up to, included some of the greatest players in league history, men such as John Devey and Jimmy Cowan (the latter with five First Division titles and two FA Cup winner's medals to his name), Howard Spencer (three First Division championships and three FA Cup medals), and Jimmy Crabtree (league championship medals with Villa in 1897, 1899 and 1900, as well as lifting the FA Cup as a part of the Aston Villa team that completed the Double in 1897). Harry Hampton, still the second-highest goalscorer for the club, was still at Villa Park when Barson joined, while Devey and Spencer were now sitting on the Villa board of directors.

Thus, in the immediate post-First World War period, Villa was still considered to be England's greatest club. It had also emerged from the Great War in reasonably good shape. Of its pre-1915 playing staff, only two men had been killed in action: Arthur Dobson, a promising young centre-half, and Tommy Barber, who had won them the cup final of 1913. Of that 1913 FA Cup side, Joe Bache, Harold Halse and Tommy Lyons had left but still on the books were keeper Sam Hardy, Tommy Weston, Jimmy Harrop, Charlie Wallace and Clem Stephenson. All were now senior players and it was around them that Ramsey and the Villa directors were attempting to build yet another successful team. Only it wasn't working out quite as expected. For the first seven weeks of the

season they had failed to win a game and it wasn't until
4 October that they earned their first two points from a
1-0 victory over Bradford. In that time they had scored
just eight goals and let in 24. It was into this crisis that
Barson now stepped.

'On 18 October, Mr Ramsey gave me instructions
to meet the Villa team the following Saturday morning
at Sheffield. They were going to Middlesbrough. I was
on the Sheffield station platform half an hour before the
Villa team arrived. When I approached the saloon door
the first man to greet me was Jimmy Harrop, the Villa
captain and a good one too. He was followed by Clem
Stephenson, the splendid inside left ...'[4]

Barson's debut was to be sensational. 'Free Lance' in
the *Sheffield Evening Telegraph* wrote:

> There were some startling results in the league
> games and first and foremost was Aston Villa's
> triumph over Middlesbrough. The advent of
> Barson will long be remembered. The Sheffield
> man simply revolutionised the play of the Villa, and
> his display was object lesson in the art of skilful
> feeding. He constantly initiated attacks and tackled
> the Middlesbro' forwards so tenaciously that they
> had to acknowledge his superiority.[5]

The *Green 'Un* reporter agreed:

> The Villa had Barson, their latest acquisition
> from Barnsley, at centre-half-back. The man who
> caused their revolution in the play was undoubtedly

Barson, whose exhibition was an object lesson in the art of skilful feeding. Time and again the Villa forwards were set in motion by brilliantly judged forward passes from the centre-half-back, whilst his determined tackling seemed to get the nerves of the Middlesbrough forwards.[6]

Barson's recollections were somewhat simpler: 'I thought the only thing to do was to stick in just as I had been doing at Barnsley. I lunged straight into the fray. I did not dally with the ball. Wherever possible I swept it out to the respective wings or pushed the ball to the inside-forwards. In the first few minutes I was fortunate in sending the ball accurately to the outside men and my success in that direction gave me any amount of confidence.'[7]

Villa would win the match 4-1 with another debutant, a local boy called Walter Boyman, scoring a hat-trick.

'They said afterwards that I played well – that I was just the man the Claret and Blues had sought. My new mates were very sporting. After the game they said, "Well played Frank." Apparently they liked the Barnsley stuff and that's all it was.'[8]

Barson was being modest, of course. He brought to the Villa team, which already possessed some very talented players, something essential.

As the game and its playing formations evolved during the 1880s, one of the two original centre-forwards slipped back into a deeper position, eventually becoming what was called a centre-half. The gradual spread of the classic 2-3-5 formation (the Pyramid) meant that this 'centre-half' soon developed into the fulcrum of the team, a figure far removed from the grim stopper he would later become.

He was a multi-skilled all-rounder, defender and attacker, leader and instigator, goalscorer and destroyer. He was, as the great Austrian football writer Willy Meisl put it, 'the most important man on the field'. The term 'pivot' described his role aptly. Possessing a man who could fulfil those duties was 'the holy grail'.[9]

The great centre-forward Steve Bloomer described the position thus in 1922:

> A half-back should be a player who is not quite forward and not quite a full-back! A centre-half should be more than this; he should be the axle on which the team revolves. His very position gives him a chance of shining simply because he is in the centre, and it is in the centre where most of the critical play takes place. Now clearing with a header, now sending his forwards away, now dropping back into the goalmouth and clearing with a hefty kick, now following his attack closely and shooting at his opponents' goal. The centre-half enjoys the attention of the crowd, and because his work is of a straightforward order gets a whole heap of praise.[10]

Barson was to be the Villa team's pivot, and perhaps even more, he was to be the driving force, the essential spark that would ignite the rest of the team. His immediate impact was just what the Villa board had paid all that money for.

Aston Villa trained on Bovril

Aston Lower Grounds,
Aston.

April 20th, 1920.

Messrs. Bovril Limited,
London.

Dear Sirs,

As trainer of the Aston Villa team,
I have much pleasure in expressing
my highest appreciation of Bovril.

The men like it, and there is no
doubt it is a very helpful addition to
their dietary in training.

Yours faithfully,
(Signed) A. MILES.

BOVRIL
gives strength to win

'In the return match at Aston against Middlesbrough we defeated the northern team again. This time the result was 5-3. In this game, which was witnessed by 45,000 people, success came my way. I was told afterwards that I had established myself as a favourite. Officials and players congratulated me on my performance. I returned to Sheffield a very proud young man. The Gods continued to be kind to me.'[11]

In fact in 21 cup and league games between 25 October and 6 March, the Villa would lose just twice when Barson was playing. It has to be said, however, that he was playing with some extremely talented men.

In goal there was Sam Hardy, already a great England international who in 24 years service to football from 1901 to 1925 notched up over 600 league appearances and boasted an impressive record of 61 clean sheets in 183 matches for Aston Villa.

Inside-forward Clem Stephenson was an expert schemer, could pass the ball with fine judgement, and was no mean goalscorer, able to shoot with both feet, pacy and was never afraid to rough it with the burly defenders.

In the first season after the war (1919/20) Stephenson was Aston Villa's top scorer with 27 goals in 39 games. During his time at Aston Villa he scored 96 goals in 216 appearances and in 1921 that visionary manager Herbert Chapman would buy him for £4,000 to lead Huddersfield Town to FA Cup and Football League titles.

Andy Ducat was an outstanding wing-half who was rarely spoken to by the referee, never booked or sent off and played the game with passion and total commitment. He would win England international honours both at soccer and cricket.

Left-half Frank Moss would partner Barson for two years and eventually rack up 283 appearances for Aston Villa as well as five England caps.

Signed along with Barson in 1919 was inside-forward Billy Kirton for a 'knock-down' price from the Leeds City club whose players had been put up for 'auction' in

October 1919 by the Football Association following the disclosure of irregularities in management.

There was right full-back Tommy Smart who was signed in January 1920, a fierce tackler whose sheer size caused apprehension to his opponents. Often described as 'barrel-chested', Smart stood 6ft 2in tall and weighed in at 13 stones 2 pounds, yet was not considered an over-robust player amongst colleagues. It was said that the presence of both Smart and Barson in the Villa's defence was enough to guarantee a Villa win against more than one side. Yet Smart was not a deliberately rough player. He possessed great positional sense, could kick and head a ball perfectly and would arrive for each match wearing a bowler hat, the last thing he took off before changing into his kit!

Finally, in the January 1920, a brilliant young player from the Black Country would make his debut: Billy Walker. In the interwar period, Walker ranked as the third member of a distinguished trio of Aston Villa's great inside-forwards, the other two being John Devey and Joe Bache. He would play a prominent part in Villa affairs over a period of 13 years. A tremendous goal-getting centre-forward, he was signed as a professional in June 1919 but made his first-team debut against Queen's Park Rangers in the first round of the 1920 FA Cup. It would be in that year's FA Cup run that Walker – and his subsequent mentor Barson – would make his name and fame.

Barson's promise that he wouldn't relinquish the 'Barnsley Punch' was kept but even his greatest advocates noticed that there was a side to his game that was regrettable. In November 1919 Aston Villa defeated Sheffield United 2-1. 'Looker On' in the *Sheffield Daily Telegraph* felt:

> The crowd enjoyed a good game but some incidents in which Kitchen, Barson and Fazackerley were concerned annoyed them. Perhaps had the referee been stricter with these players they would have curbed their temper. They were fortunate not to be ordered off while there was no possible excuse for Fazackerley when he attempted to trip the referee. Such behaviour as this warrants drastic punishment. Harrop was perhaps the best of the Villa half-backs, Ducat was somewhat slow, while Barson spoiled much good work by foul play and tendency to try and bluff the referee when meted out the slightest charge.[12]

Barson, as usual, professed to be careless of such criticism: 'Now and again the critics had a dig at me. At some of our away matches I came in for adverse comment. On one occasion, I believe it was at White Hart Lane, I heard a spectator call out to me as we were leaving the field at the interval, "Ere, Barson, not so many of those Barnsley tricks – play the game!" Oh well, that did not discourage me. I kept pegging away ... '[13]

His aggression and drive would eventually pay off for Villa as he propelled them forward, Barnsley-style, to the culmination of an FA Cup Final triumph. Before that, however, his nation would come calling.

Endnotes

1. *Athletic News*, 28 April 1924
2. *Sports Argus*, 27 August 1960
3. Mems
4. Ditto
5. *Sheffield Evening Telegraph*, 27 October 1919
6. *Star Green 'Un*, 1 November 1919
7. Mems
8. Mems
9. Jonathan Wilson *Inverting the Pyramid*, (London: Orion, 2013) (general references)
10. *Derbyshire Advertiser and Journal*, 9 September 1922
11. Mems
12. *Sheffield Daily Telegraph*, 24 November 1919
13. Mems

Chapter Eight

An England Cap

'Had Barson been encouraged in his international ambitious, had he won the honours that his talents deserve, he might have been a different character today. England also would probably be holding her head much higher in the football world.' **Steve Bloomer, Derbyshire Advertiser and Journal, Friday, 30 April 1926.**

'The crowd at Selhurst Park shouted for Barson and Bedford! Did the selectors hear them, and if so, will they heed them? The obvious first choice for centre-half is Barson; he is without peer as a footballer, and on merit and talent alone walks into any English side. But if the selectors are so biased and so prejudiced that they will not have Barson at any price, then surely the next best thing ought to be the choice.' **Derby Daily Telegraph, 13 March 1926.**

BEING SELECTED to play for England between the two wars was a hit-and-miss business. England 'boasted' a 14-man international selection committee that often seemed intent on playing anyone but the best players. Throughout the interwar period there were complaints that the committee was too large, too old and too out of touch. They rarely met at 'trial' games, and when choosing a team there was a great deal of cross-voting and the pressing of home-club 'favourites' by individual committee members.

There were also only three official 'caps' on offer per season: those against the Scots, Welsh and Irish. There was no European Championship and no World Cup. FIFA was formed in 1905 but England withdrew in 1920, re-entered in 1924 and left again in 1928. It would not enter the World Cup until 1950. There were occasional FA Tours abroad as well as inter-league matches but the Home International Tournament was what counted.

The means by which a player gained selection was via yearly trial matches, usually held in January or February. They were unpopular because the weather was generally poor, the ground inconveniently situated for players to reach on a Monday afternoon and the selected teams were thrown together without preparation. However, just to be chosen for a 'trial' was in itself an honour.

As early as 1920, Barson was being considered as a potential England centre-back. His elevation to the First Division and Aston Villa ensured that he would be considered, but his international career would be brief.

Barson wrote: 'I figured in the trial matches – South versus England at the Hawthorns and England versus the

North at Newcastle. In the trial match at the Hawthorns on 9 February I was in the wars. I finished up with a lovely black eye and a rather badly damaged nose, although I was able to turn out for the Villa the following Saturday. The injuries were the result of an accidental collision with Joe McCall ...'[1]

Barson's inclusion in a squad representing the South was slightly odd and it suggested that he was not going to be first choice. Joe McCall of Preston North End was opposite him and considered by many to be the man in possession, although he'd been capped just three times before the war and was 34 years old.

The first trial took place on 9 February at West Bromwich Albion's ground in front of 12,000 spectators, with an England 11 playing a team composed of players drawn from the south. There was a high wind blowing that mitigated against good football and though the game was contested with great keenness, play was not of a high class. Centre-half Joe McCall's wing colleagues in the England 11, Andy Ducat and Arthur Grimsdell, 'were inclined to bunch at times, whilst the latter also hung on to the ball too much in the second half. But for all that, they always had something in hand, and possessed subtlety of movement that Smith, Barson, and Barton lacked, well though these three played.'[2]

Barson 'delighted his admirers with a polished exhibition – but came off worse after a collision with Preston's McCall and went off with ten minutes to go'.[3]

It seemed his chance had gone, but another trial was arranged for late February and when Watson dropped out of the North side Barson replaced him. He did well, playing out of position, but wasn't considered to have done enough to displace McCall, who played for the opposing England 11.

There was already some debate in the newspapers concerning his eligibility for the England role. The *Lancashire Evening Post* correspondent suggested that Barson's case was being 'pushed by a well-known Manchester critic'. He went on to suggest that Joe McCall wasn't liked in Manchester because he'd kept Charlie Roberts of Manchester United out of the side before the war. 'Until McCall is seen to be on the decline, Barson cannot live with him. The North-ender will be amused that he is thought lacking in muscularity.'[4] *The Globe* correspondent begged to differ: McCall had, like William Wedlock, had his innings. 'Barson is his natural successor, and cannot be kept out of the team for any but sentimental reasons. He won his place fairly and squarely at The Hawthorns when, with an infinitely more difficult task, he outshone the Preston captain. It was not until he left the field injured that the England team registered the winning goal. Truth to tell, there are not many problems to disturb the rest of the selectors. Without any qualms these names can be set down before any serious thinking is done: Hardy, Pennington, Grimsdell, Barson, Morris, Cock, Buchan.'[5]

The Globe was correct, initially. When the team was announced for the forthcoming match against Wales, Barson was centre-half. He was partnered in the half-back line by team-mate Andy Ducat and Spurs' Arthur Grimsdell. Up front was Charles Buchan and in goal team-mate Sam Hardy. It was hardly a team for the future, however: England would have six players over 30, Hardy aged 37 and Pennington 36, with Alf Quantrill the youngest at 23.

And so, on 15 March 1920 at Arsenal's Highbury Stadium, Frank Barson ran out wearing his England shirt – the one and only time he would be privileged to do so.

Early morning snow had completely spoiled the pitch, apparently, which had puddles plentifully distributed over its surface, but the weather kept fine during the game and there were about 22,000 people present. England took the lead after seven minutes' play. Jesse Pennington placed the ball from a free kick across the field, and Buchan, having dribbled neatly in order to find an opening, shot clear of Peers into the net. It was to be England's only highlight. The *Sheffield Daily Telegraph* reporter noted:

> … with play going more evenly than at the start, the Welsh left-wing ran down and Pennington handled in the penalty area. Davies took the kick and beat Hardy with a powerful shot … The game became more open after this, and, in the course of a Welsh attack, Clay put the ball back with the intention of leaving Pennington an easy clearance. Instead, the ball rolled slowly and Richards dashed up to tackle, first the full-back and then Hardy, who had run out of goal. Forward and goalkeeper both stumbled, but Richards kept his feet, got the ball from Hardy's hands, and proceeded to kick through an open goal.[6]

With the ground starting to cut up badly, the Welsh won 2-1, 44-year-old Billy Meredith featuring prominently for Wales. According to *The Times*, it was a delay in finishing attacks and uncertainty in defence that accounted for England's defeat.

It was to be Billy Meredith's last appearance for his country and a truly fitting climax to his long career. Richards and Davies scored the Welsh goals and if Meredith's own part was less dramatic he had achieved the victory he had dreamt of for almost 30 years. Afterwards, in the dressing room, they said that he wept unashamedly. He was entitled to his tears. It had, after all, been a long and difficult trail.

By stark contrast, Barson's trail had ended almost before it had begun. Perseus in the *Lancashire Evening Post* summed him up:

MEN WHO FAILED

One does not envy the selectors their task. Several of the XI that did duty yesterday let them down badly.

I should not disturb the half-back line, except to reinstate McCall, who certainly should not have been left out for Barson. The Villa man is undeniably a good, workmanlike player, and an improving one in his present company, but he is not the finished schemer, the constructive force, that the North-Ender is, and too much his work, yesterday, was spoilt by passes that did not reach their objective.[7]

Along with his fellow half-backs, he was said to have, 'supported the forwards admirably and assisted in frequent attacks', but he never played for England again. He was dropped for the forthcoming England versus Scotland game, Joe McCall replacing him for the latter's first appearance in six years. England would secure a rare victory over Scotland (5-4) but would field their oldest-ever side with six men in their 30s.

Sheffield Wednesday's George Wilson would take the centre-half spot in 1921 for the next few years. Considered by some to be the greatest centre-half-back the club had had since the days of Tom Crawshaw, he would earn a dozen caps and captain England five times, but England would struggle over the next seven to eight years, winning just six out of 24 full Home International matches. Wilson would be on the winning side just four times.

Steve Bloomer, one of England's greatest forwards, thought dropping Barson was a mistake:

> To tell the honest truth, Barson, in my opinion, has no peer at centre-half today in the United Kingdom and Ireland. George Wilson [Wednesday] and Max Woosnam [Manchester City] are two sterling players but Barson is pre-eminent. There is no player today who can bring a high ball down to the carpet and keep it there as can Barson. There is no centre-half who can keep away from the backs, giving them a clear space in which to operate and at the same time play wonderful defensive work as does Barson. His initiation, ground passing,

heading and generalship are of the highest order. There is a player who could subdue Andrew Wilson and yet find time to feed his forwards. It is the highest praise I can give Barson.[8]

When Wilson eventually stepped down it was expected by many that Barson would take his place, but it was not to be. The England selectors went for Burnley's Townrow in 1926, and 'Old Cap' writing in the *Lancashire Daily Post* was scathing after yet another England defeat, this time at the hands of Wales – again.

> I don't quite know why Townrow was there. He is poor successor to Joe McCall and George Wilson, while Frank Barson would eat his head off in hard and crucial games. It seems strange that either the selection committee should be ignorant of the latter's commanding ability, else should allow some petty prejudice to operate adversely to him. If he is good enough to play in league football, he ought to be enough to play for his country.[9]

The continued non-selection of Barson would become almost a scandal in the 1920s. It cannot have helped Barson's outlook and attitude towards football's authorities.

The 'petty prejudice' explaining why Barson would remain unconsidered by England's hierarchy for the rest of his long career may well have had its origins in his clashes with the Aston Villa board, which would begin almost immediately following his first triumphant season at Villa Park. Before then, however, Barson would experience his finest moment as a player – when making an FA Cup Final appearance.

Villa began their campaign with a 2-1 victory over Queens Park Rangers. They would then take on Manchester United and the ageless Billy Meredith. It was a tough game, although the ramifications of this game would eventually go well beyond the football pitch.

United led 1-0 at half-time, with Meredith providing trademark pin-point crosses and corner-kicks. In the second half, however, Villa and Barson gradually took control.

'A heavy challenge between the tall Barson and the sturdy diminutive Meehan knocked the life out of the most vigorous of the United forwards. Barson, at centre-half, was a tower of strength both in attack and defence, and he reduced Woodcock to a mere passenger.'[10]

Goals from Stephenson and Walker saw Villa prevail 2-1 but Meredith would have his revenge on Barson the following month.

However, there was a backstory to the match that would come back to haunt Barson. Some days later, the following item appeared in a Birmingham paper:

VILLA PLAYERS LONG WALK

Two of Aston Villa's most prominent players, Hardy the goalkeeper, and Barson the centre-half – had a narrow escape of missing the cup-tie with Manchester United at Trafford Park on Saturday in extraordinary circumstances. The players during the morning were proceeding from their homes to Manchester when their train was held up by the collision which occurred between a slow train from Sheffield and a goods train at a point between Godley and Mottram.

There was nothing for them to do but to walk to Stalybridge, a distance of seven miles, in order to get another train. They accomplished this tramp, and ultimately arrived in Manchester and reached the ground about a quarter of an hour before the kick-off. Their experience fortunately did not affect their form, as Hardy saved his goal brilliantly in the first half-minute of the game, while Barson took a leading part in the victory over the United.[11]

In his memoirs, Barson dramatised the incident somewhat:

'We got onto the main road. We had no difficulty in finding the way but the weather! – it was fierce. We trudged on and on into the teeth of the driving wind and sleet. Within ten minutes we were wet to the skin – we were nice beauties for a cup tie, if we could ever get to it! We were always hoping that a motor-car would come in sight or a motor-lorry; indeed any sort of vehicle. But our luck was clean out. Some cars did pass us but the drivers did not respond to our frantic signals. I suppose they thought we were a couple of tramps. So – like poor old Felix but not quite so happy as that quaint little customer – we kept on walking.'[12]

After various adventures, such as unsuccessfully offering a man with a horse and cart £20 to get them to their destination, they reached Stalybridge – 'cold, wet, hungry, tired and thoroughly depressed'.

There they found a coffee stall, had coffee and 'well-buttered rolls', then caught a tramcar to the station. They caught the train and were at Victoria Station but with only 20 minutes to kick-off. There were no taxis. The football rush to Old Trafford was on. But Hardy espied a motor-van and knew the driver. He agreed to take them and they arrived at Old Trafford with seven minutes to kick-off.

'We rushed through the official entrance in whirlwind fashion nearly knocking over several people in the corridor, dashed into the dressing room and proved to be, I am certain, the quickest quick-change artistes ever seen in a dressing room.'[13]

All very amusing for Barson, but for the Villa directors something of a shock. (As Barson conceded, 'but our narrow shave had worried the Villa directorate'.) It would continue to worry them.

In round three, it was Sunderland who were defeated 1-0, the goal coming from an increasingly effective Clem Stephenson. According to Jimmy Catton in *Athletic News*, however, man of the match was Barson:

BARSON'S BRILLIANCE

Barson stood head and shoulders above every other player and if one man can win a football match he can. I confess that I do not like to see a centre-half adopt such a risky proceeding as to heel a ball but once he did so with perfect accuracy. Barson has been trained in a school where cup-tie fighting is characteristic of the side and he has learned the whole art. He knows how to make the most of his splendid physique. Although he receives as well as he gives, the only fault I could possibly find with Barson was that he was rather too vigorous, as Buchan could testify for twice he was curled up on the floor. With quite a heavy charge, Barson heaved Buchan over the touch-line early in the game. A free kick was given because he was unnecessarily violent and this incident seemed to take some of the pith out of Buchan's legs. Buchan is a man of superior strength to most players and it would be well for him to remember that the first principle of charging is to nudge the opponent off the ball, and not to incapacitate him.[14]

Barson himself recalled, 'As Buchan went down, he said I was the best dirty player he'd ever played against. I said he was the biggest baby I'd ever known. But I still regarded Charlie as one of the finest inside-forwards I knew and we were the best of pals …'[15]

Buchan himself never referred to the incident directly, but he seemed sanguine enough when writing his biography:

> Soccer in the old days was tougher and one got more hard shakings from charges and strong tackles, but serious injuries were fewer then than they are now. Once you were free of an opponent, there was little fear he would bring you down from behind. In fact, it was something of a 'cold war' in those far-off days. Players tried to frighten you off your game but their bark was much worse than their bite.[16]

In March it was Tottenham Hotspur at White Hart Lane where Villa triumphed somewhat fortuitously, courtesy of an own goal conceded by Tommy Clay, the Londoners' right-back, who turned the ball into the net while attempting what seemed to be a harmless clearance. Spurs apparently outplayed and overwhelmed Villa but could not score.

Observers felt that it had been Barson who'd probably saved his side by the way in which he'd held up Jimmy Cantrell, Spurs' veteran but high-scoring centre-forward. Cantrell was almost a decade older than Barson and would gain his revenge the following season when Spurs defeated Villa and went on to lift the cup.

In the semi-final at Bramall Lane in 1920, Villa came up against Chelsea, who were in the unique position of knowing that, if they won, they would appear in the final on their own home pitch, Stamford Bridge. But this eventuality never arose for Villa won 3-1 and Billy Walker, who had by now succeeded Harry Hampton at centre-forward, scored two of the goals. It was a tough game, during which Walker was twice knocked out and twice carried off, only to return soon afterwards. It also witnessed one of the 1920s most glamorous players pitched against the least likely of all poster boys.

Owing to his good looks and a tenor voice, Chelsea's Jack Cock would appear regularly on the music hall stage. In fact, even during his playing days he was renowned for singing before entering the pitch. The best-dressed footballer of his day, with show-business connections and a war-time Military Medal to his name, he appeared in several films and had his own column in *The Globe* evening newspaper. None of this availed him when he confronted Barson.

Jimmy Catton considered the 'eclipse' of Cock 'remarkable'. 'I have rarely seen him exert so little influence on a game. Barson blotted him out completely.' Catton criticised Cock for allowing himself to become rattled: 'A footballer of his position should not allow himself to be disturbed either by Barson or a referee's decisions. At one point Cock folded his arms in contempt when the ref refused a claim.' Cock was thus shut out of the game entirely by Barson, who seemed to enjoy pitting himself against England's premier players.

'Barson shadowed Cock all over the ground. He never gave the Chelsea centre the least latitude until the issue was safe. The ex-Barnsley man, however, was more than a mere spoiler. Of course, it was an achievement to render this forward harmless, but Barson was a constructive player. He was excellent in heading and in distributing passes to such advantage that he was a universal helper. At times Barson was inclined to be too keen, for in a cup tie he is in his element as one who never spares either himself or his antagonist. For such a game there are very few more resolute and more calculating players.'[17]

Other critics agreed, although there seemed to be some slight misgivings concerning Barson's methods. Perseus in the *Lancashire Evening Post* felt that Barson's 'strong, ruthless methods do not quite fit with the Villa style and should have been punished oftener'.[18] While the *Sheffield Daily Telegraph*'s 'Looker On' noted, 'Another outstanding figure was Barson, and it is a pity that so

capable a player should mar his play by foul tactics. In this game he reduced Cock to absolute impotency, and the Chelsea leader had a very dismal time – Barson is a great man at smashing attacks and can also keep his forwards on the go.'[19]

Unfortunately for Barson, his violent eclipsing of various prominent English players had not gone unnoticed by football's authorities.

Endnotes
1. Mems
2. *Nottingham Journal* , 10 February 1920
3. *Birmingham Daily Gazette*, 10 February 1920
4. *Lancashire Evening Post*, 28 February 1920
5. *The Globe*, 3 March 1920
6. *Sheffield Daily Telegraph*, Tuesday, 16 March 1920
7. *Lancashire Evening Post*, Tuesday, 16 March 1920
8. *Sheffield Independent*, 21 March 1922
9. *Lancashire Daily Post*, 20 March 1926
10. *Sunday Post*, Sunday, 1 February 1920
11. *Birmingham Daily Gazette*, Monday, 2 February 1920
12. Mems
13. Ditto
14. *Athletic News*, 21 February 1920
15. Mems
16. Charles Buchan, *A Lifetime In Football* (The Sportsman's Book Club, 1956)
17. *Athletic News*, 29 March 1920
18. *Lancashire Evening Post*, 29 March 1920
19. *Sheffield Daily Telegraph*, Monday, 29 March 1920

Chapter Nine

A Cup Final Warning

'Jack Howcroft had a very comfortable task in controlling the match as befitted a man of his experience. Only once had he to administer a lecture and that was when Barson first did something that did not square with fair play and then talked too much ...' **Perseus, *Lancashire Evening Post*, Monday, 26 April 1920.**

'I'm not a lover of the self-advertising referee – the man who had got a whistle and used it like a child did a plaything ... I have seen some referees who ought to have been with Barnum and Baily's Show. The attitudes they struck on the field would make one think they were training on the football field for tragedians on the stage.' **C.E. Sutcliffe, *Burnley News*, 24 February 1923.**

THE 1920 cup final hasn't gone down in history as a classic. The first final since the end of the war, it took place at Chelsea's ground at Stamford Bridge, the change of venue being lamented by *The Times* as eliminating the 'bean-feast' atmosphere of the usual venue, Crystal Palace, with its accompanying fairground. It was, 'just like any other cup tie'.[1]

Even the fans who travelled down from the north seemed unlike those who normally thronged the capital on cup final day, a consequence, one correspondent thought, of the recent Great War:

> The Huddersfield and Brummagem spectators kept up the final traditions by arriving early, wearing their colours and walking or driving all over town. But to London eyes they seemed far less barbaric than the excursionists who came up for pre-war final ties. They were well dressed, sober, and quiet. The majority wore bowlers or soft felt hats, and their clothes were not markedly unlike the London cut. London, which affects to regard the men of the Midlands and the north as another race, is rather piqued at the change. One noticed, too, that the visitors knew their way about very well and did not take the Law Courts for Buckingham Palace. That, after all, is not surprising. Most of them have been here quite lately, but in khaki.[2]

Nevertheless, there was still tremendous interest in the event, and even though only 50,000 saw the game, many

Grimesthorpe Works, Charles Cammell and Co. Ltd where Frank Barson spent many years from age 12 through the First World War working as a blacksmith. **Sheffield Libraries and Archives**

Draper Street from Carlisle Road showing the Hodson Hotel (left) looking towards Adsetts Street and Grimesthorpe Works. **David Ainscough**

Carlisle Road, Grimesthorpe looking towards Carlisle Street East. Frank lived on both roads before moving to Manchester in 1927. **David Ainscough**

Grimesthorpe County School, Earl Marshal Road and the junction with Grimesthorpe Road where Frank Barson rarely went. **Courtesy of Sheffield Libraries and Archives**

The Wentworth Café (foreground) where Frank Barson came face to face with Charles Clegg for his first ever suspension April 1912. **Courtesy of Sheffield Libraries and Archives**

Making laminated railway springs, where Frank Barson and family members worked – taken from the brochure of the visit of George V and Queen Mary to Cammell Laird, Grimesthorpe Steel and Ordnance Works. **Courtesy of Sheffield Libraries and Archives**

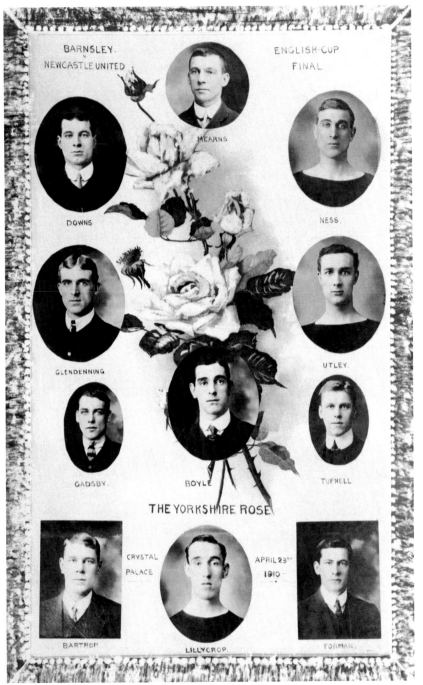

The 'Barnsley Battlers', the Barnsley team that reached the FA Cup Final in 1910. They were the inspiration for Frank Barson's entire career. **Getty**

1920 FA Cup Final. Stamford Bridge, London 24 April, 1920. Aston Villa v Huddersfield Town. Prince Henry meets the Aston Villa team before the match. Frank Barson is on extreme right with an very modern hairstyle. **Getty**

Aston Villa, 1920 FA Cup winners. Frank Barson is on the front row, second left. **Colorsport**

The Manchester United squad that Frank Barson led into the First Division in 1925.

27 March 1926: Roberts of Manchester City scores from a corner kick against Manchester United in the FA Cup semi-final. **Getty**

Frank Barson (on right) signs for young fans.
Author

Barson proudly wearing his England shirt. **Author**

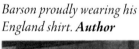

Frank Barson (far right) at the Alexander Sports Ground in 1938 with Aston Villa trainees. **Dean Beresford**

Frank Barson (on left with ball) along with Joe Beresford (far right) coaching the young Aston Villa players. **Dean Beresford**

Frank Barson in 1954.
Colorsport

Frank (third from left, back row) with his Swansea City players at the start of the 1947/48 season.

Back (left to right): Thomas Keane, James Feeney, Frank Barson (trainer), Reginald Weston, John 'Jack' Parry, Roy Paul, W. McCandless (manager), Francis Burns.

Front: E. Payne, Samuel McCrory, Raymond Powell, Francis Scine, William Morris.

staying away because they believed they would be crushed, the receipts constituted a new record of £9,722, 10s.

Villa's rather downbeat preparations for what was a record sixth appearance in cup finals involved *not* going

Aston Villa FA Cup winning side cigarette card

away nor engaging in 'special training'; instead, the team remained at Villa Park, their only departure from the normal schedule being to take regular walks to local Sutton Park and back, plus occasional trips to Droitwich brine baths.

Huddersfield, newly promoted and underrated and attempting to become the first club to achieve promotion and win the cup in the same season, were pinning their hopes on the influence of an Aladdin's lamp, procured from a local pantomime and present at all their matches that season. The players apparently gathered round it before each game and rubbed it for luck. Alas, Aladdin deserted them and even dealt them a slice of bad luck in the shape of a 'fluke' goal.

Typical headlines following Villa's 1-0 victory said it all: 'A Staid Final' (*Daily Herald*) and 'Fluky Goal in Extra Time gives Villa the Cup' (*Green 'Un*, 24 April)

The goal in question came from dashing Villa forward Billy Kirton in the seventh minute of extra time – the first occasion that the additional period had been played in a final. Villa's winger Arthur Dorrell won a corner and sent across a ball that hung tantalisingly in front of goal. Kirton and Wilson, the Huddersfield centre-half, went up for it together, Kirton getting there first and sending the ball into the net via Wilson's face.

It was sufficient to win Villa the match, although Huddersfield came desperately near equalising in the closing minutes. The game was played in sweltering conditions and the extra half hour – a surprise to many, including some of the players who complained to the referee about it – took its toll. The *Liverpool Echo* reporter sympathised:

> Had you been there reader you would have felt sorry for the players. At every chance they popped to the touchline to get a drink from the ambulance men's satchels and when there was a stoppage every man had a suck at the trainer's sponge. Thirst, well, that was not the word for it. The pace of the game was certainly a cracker ...[3]

Barson himself had little to say about the match in his 1925 memoirs, except that it was 'the most strenuous of my career'. In later years, however, he would float a story that he had been unfairly treated by the referee, in this case the 'famous' Mr J.T. Howcroft.

In a series written for *Charles Buchan's Football Monthly* in 1956, Barson declared,

> I must be the only man who was ever cautioned about his conduct before going out to play in a

Daily Mail *cartoon*

cup final. After getting changed Sam Hardy, that prince of goalkeepers, and myself were listening to the band entertaining the spectators before the kick-off. As we sat there, the famous referee J.T. Howcroft walked up and said he had come to caution me about my play that afternoon. As I sat there open-mouthed, he went on, 'The first wrong move you make this afternoon, Barson – off you go!' What an introduction to the biggest game of all ...[4]

He elaborated on the tale a few years later when writing about the incident in Birmingham's *Sports Argus*

... my enthusiasm landed me in trouble right from
the word 'go'. A cup final appearance is every
player's dream – yet even that day was marred for
me. As we sat there Jack Howcroft – rated one of
the finest ever referees – but not by me – walked up
and said: 'THE FIRST WRONG MOVE YOU
MAKE THIS AFTERNOON, BARSON. OFF
YOU GO!' I couldn't believe my ears at first ...
then I told him where to go in language which
certainly wouldn't be used at a vicarage garden
party ...[5]

The only corroboration for Barson's story was provided by
team-mate Frank Moss a year later: 'Before the game he
[FB] was given a lecture by the referee, Jack Howcroft,
as he has already told you in his own articles. I couldn't
believe my ears when I heard Howcroft say to Frank, "Any
trouble from you Barson and off you'll go," I thought it
was a shocking thing to say to any man before a final.'[6]

Moss isn't perhaps the most reliable of witnesses,
however. Fred Archer, the Aston Villa secretary for almost
50 years, also repeated the story some eight years later in
1969, although he put it slightly differently, suggesting
that Barson had been 'warned' about his conduct rather
than officially cautioned.

The term 'caution' must be understood in a completely
different context to today's. In the 1920s referees certainly
'cautioned' players for foul play but it was often hard to
know whether they were simply telling the man off or
issuing a more formal reprimand as now when cards
would be shown. What's more, until 1922 referees were

under no obligation to report the incident to the Football Association.

Two such 'cautions' still meant dismissal from the game, of course, although it sometimes came as a surprise to a player who hadn't realised, in the heat of battle, that the referee had officially sanctioned him.

While there's a distinct possibility that Barson was dramatising something for effect (the reference to his heated response seems unlikely bearing in mind the type of man Howcroft was), a closer look at the game itself suggests that something odd did happen at some point. There is also the question of exactly who the referee was and why he had been selected for this particular match.

It had been expected that referee Harry Rylance, who'd officiated in the Chelsea–Villa semi-final, was going to be the official in charge, but in April in the 'Chatter' column of the *Lancashire Evening Post*, there appeared a hint as to why he would eventually be passed over:

> Harry Rylance, the Lancashire cricket scorer, was popularly supposed to go right through the cup-final rounds to the final, but he stopped short at the semi-final, in which he allowed Barson a little too much rope over his methods. But the rope hanged Rylance's chance – not Barson's.[7]

As we have seen, Villa's progress to the final had been characterised by Barson's successful 'dismantling' of top players such as Charles Buchan and Jack Cock. While he hadn't committed any specific offences, his methods had been considered by some as regrettable, possibly even 'unsportsmanlike'. Cock had certainly thought so, and would subsequently write in his *Globe* newspaper column:

> I cannot understand why footballers should adopt rough tactics on the field. The game is a living to us and it is not up to us as sportsmen to try to knock brother professionals out. By receiving a serious knock one may lose one's bread and butter and I for one should regret it for the rest of my life if I were responsible for anything like that, even by accident.[8]

Referee Jack Howcroft was something of a 'celebrity' referee, distinctive in his style of dress (he always wore a little black cap) and the flamboyant manner in which he controlled games. Don Davis, the veteran sports writer, summed him up thus: 'The complete master of the grand manner. To men like J.T. Howcroft refereeing was life; unceasingly he studied the part, rehearsed the part, acted the part; and one feels sure that he took no share in a game without believing that of 25 performers involved (including the linesmen) the greatest of these was Howcroft.'

'BC' in the *Green 'Un* dubbed him,

> The Hamlet of Bolton because that's how cartoonists tended to depict him, with his distinctive style of pointing in dramatic fashion whenever giving a decision. He always strikes the onlooker as a man who is not likely to put up with any nonsense and I know that he strikes the players

that way, too, for some of them have told me so …
He is the soundest referee in the country.[9]

Howcroft was a controversial figure, however, and tended to the belief that he knew better than the legislators. He agreed with Charles Buchan that the sliding tackle was 'dangerous' even though the FA rule book stated that it wasn't, 'if properly made to take the ball and not the man'.

Howcroft considered that impossible. 'Football players should play the ball when on their feet and not when they are lying on or sliding along the ground, having got there for the specific purpose of taking an unfair advantage …' Thus, he always blew for a foul if the player went to ground: 'In my days as a referee I never hesitated to penalise any form of so-called sliding tackle and was never taken to task for so doing.'[10]

His pedantic adherence to the rule book might well have derived from his early days as a referee. He began officiating as long ago as 1900 and in 1905 found himself suspended for a month for failing to control both players and crowd during a match between Everton and Manchester United. This was one of the notorious games that saw Billy Meredith and the Manchester club heavily punished for a variety of misdemeanours. Howcroft was determined never to make the mistake again.

Professional players differed in their assessments of him. Veteran England centre-half Willie Wedlock considered the 1920 cup final players lucky to have him in control: 'Mr Howcroft from the start was out to check anything and everything that might lead to dangerous or ungentlemanly conduct.'[11] Frank Moss, by contrast, wrote: 'Many rate Howcroft as the finest ever referee, but in my opinion he was too fond of stressing his own personality and he was often too far behind the play.'[12] A 1925 *Thomson's Weekly News* profile agreed with Moss: 'Very rarely was Mr Howcroft seen running up the field to keep in touch with the play. When the centre of activity changed he strode over the turf at a walking pace.'

There was also some official disapproval of him. C.E. Sutcliffe was a member of the Football League Management Committee, a Burnley FC director and had been a referee since 1891, the year of Barson's birth. He was also a founder and the first president of the Referees' Association. In 1923 Sutcliffe mocked Howcroft indirectly: 'The continual pointing and wagging of the finger and the attitudes they struck make one wonder whether they were referees or acrobats.'

In 1925 Sutcliffe took Howcroft to task by suggesting that the man's ideas on refereeing represented, 'a real source of danger to referees … He is sweeping aside with the utmost nonchalance instruction which we have accepted for our guidance and enunciating new ideas that will assuredly terminate prematurely the careers of those who unfortunately adopt them.'

He added, 'Whether 22 players leave the field injured or not is generally a matter of good fortune and no matter how strict a referee may be or how anxious players may be to avoid injury, the latter arises without blame attaching to anyone … It is no consolation to a club that loses points through mistakes by the referee to say, "Oh, but all your men have escaped injury and see how good-tempered they are!"'[13]

Nevertheless, it would appear that Howcroft had been assigned the cup final with an agenda: to curb Barson at the first opportunity. A number of football correspondents noted his immediate impact:

'There was an incident when Mann ran and dispossessed Barson calmly as you please, when the pivot was sauntering forward. Barson didn't like it and expressed his opinions about the business so loudly that referee Howcroft stopped the game and admonished him. It was a rebuke which attracted all eyes to Barson.'[14]

'After half an hour of strenuous football, the first foul occurred and referee Howcroft was emphatic in demonstrating his disapproval of Barson's infringement ...'[15]

'Barson was spotted by the referee when doing a trick not allowed by the rules called aside and cautioned by the referee and a free kick awarded.'[16]

Barson later insisted that Howcroft's close attentions, 'didn't stop me playing my usual game'. Once again, this isn't quite true.

Jack Howcroft cigarette card

Frank Moss thought, 'Howcroft's wigging upset Frank a little and though he didn't play badly he was not quite his usual brilliant form in the first half against Huddersfield. He was simply too frightened to tackle anyone.'[17]

'Touchstone' in the *Birmingham Daily Gazette* agreed:

The tall centre half has frequently played much better than on this occasion. A word from the referee early in the game when his excitement caused him to be a little too vigorous with Swann seemed to upset him badly and he was half afraid to exercise his usual high spirits. Nevertheless, Barson was an important factor in a great line, especially during that extra half hour when he played with a greater determination than any other man on the field.[18]

Jack Swann himself later recalled the incident: 'The funniest moment was when Frank Barson tried to get me. He was the most banned player of the day and I think he was after my body! The referee Jack Howcroft saw him and said, "No more of that Barson," and he didn't get me after all.'[19]

In his *Thomson's Weekly News* reminisces a couple of years later, Howcroft made no mention of his reprimanding of Barson, either before or during the game. In fact, he claimed the game had been completely foul-free. He did describe, however, that after the match he visited the two dressing rooms, telling the Villa players they were lucky to have won and congratulating the Huddersfield players, whom he clearly considered the more worthy team.

Barson revealed that Howcroft repeated the pre-match threat to him some years later when officiating in another Villa game. 'It wasn't the last of my clashes with Mr. Howcroft. I was not afraid of any man, yet I must confess I dropped out of a side due to play at Blackpool when I heard Howcroft was the referee. I felt certain he would have sent me off had I played.'[20]

At the end of the game, the cup was duly presented to the Villa players by Prince Henry, son of King George. There were no speeches, just three cheers for the prince led by the FA Secretary F.J. Wall. The Prince raised his hat in acknowledgement, shook his head when asked to speak and left in his motorcar.

At the banquet later that evening, the president of the Football League, Mr J. McKenna, essayed a topical joke, referring to the Villa as the 'gramophone club' because they were 'always setting up new records'.

Sunday was spent at Brighton and on the Monday the Villa players returned to Birmingham, but not before visiting a nursing home where one of the team, Edgley, was recovering from a broken leg that had kept him out of the game.

'The English Cup was taken to him, and some champagne put in it, and he had a drink from the cup. The doctor and nurses also had a drink, being very pleased to have the opportunity. Immediately afterwards the party made its way to Euston in order to commence the journey to Birmingham so as to fulfil their League engagement with Manchester City in the evening.'[21]

Back in Birmingham, there was the traditional railway station welcome:

'As soon as they emerged from New Street Station the men were literally overwhelmed by the enthusiasts, who pressed round to tender their congratulations, and their progress to Aston was a triumphant procession.'[22]

The game against Manchester City proved something of an anti-climax, Villa losing by the only goal and Barson missing a penalty! Even the glittering presence of the FA Cup, which Ducat had brought on to the field, could not inspire the Aston men and a crowd of 45,000 went home disappointed.

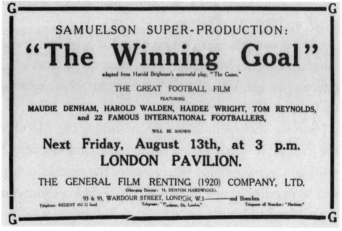

The Winning Goal *film poster*

There were few if any rewards on offer for cup winners in 1920, apart from the regulation fee for a final. A nationwide advert for Alkia Saltrates and Reudal Bath Saltrates to help with muscular aches, pains and foot troubles mentioned Barson and the Villa players but one can assume they were paid nothing at all, apart from perhaps some free packets to put in their foot baths.[23]

During the summer of 1920, however, Barson was invited along with Ducat, Hardy and Stephenson to act as football-playing extras for a new film, *The Winning Goal*, adapted from Harold Brighouse's play *The Game*. They assembled at the Birmingham Stadium and were drilled into performing, 'a number of characteristic scenes illustrating incidents in the game'. Later in the year they were invited to a screening at the Scala, where Barson was reacquainted with Jack Cock, who had a part in the film.

By that time, however, Barson and Stephenson were making headlines of their own.

Endnotes
1. *The Times*, 23 April 1920
2. *Sheffield Daily Telegraph*, 26 April 1920
3. *Liverpool Echo*, 26 April 1920
4. *Charles Buchan's Football Monthly*, September to December 1956
5. *Sports Argus*, 27 August 1960
6. *Sports Argus*, 8 April 1961
7. *Lancashire Evening Post*, 3 April 1920
8. *The Globe*, 4 December 1920
9. *Star Green 'Un*, 13 December 1913
10. *Star Green 'Un*, 9 January 1937
11. *Cambridge Independent Press*, 28 April 1920
12. *Sports Argus*, 8 April 1961
13. *Liverpool Echo*, 3 October 1925
14. *Star Green 'Un*, 24 April 1920
15. *Daily Mail*, 24 October 1920
16. *Sunday Post*, 25 April 1920
17. *Sports Argus*, 8 April 1961
18. *Birmingham Daily Gazette*, 26 April 1920
19. *Sportsmail*, 1981
20. Mems
21. *Birmingham Daily Gazette*, 27 April 1920
22. *Birmingham Daily Gazette*, 27 April 1920
23. *Coventry Evening Telegraph*, 22 March 1921

Chapter Ten

The Stormy Petrel of the Game

'Frank Barson and Clem Stephenson, of Aston Villa, have been suspended for a fortnight for not turning up and refusing to play in the league match at Bolton on 15 September, and have been given a month's time to arrange for going to live in Birmingham. Their suspension dates from 16th to the 30th.' **The Burnley News, Saturday, 25 September 1920.**

HIS FIRST successful season with Aston Villa should have been the start of a glorious top-class career for Frank Barson. Not only had he won one of the game's most prestigious prizes, but his dynamic early season play had also led to him earning an England cap, something many of his admirers had long prophesied. Alas, nothing ever seemed to run smoothly for Barson and within a few months of being presented with his precious cup medal by Prince Henry he was embroiled in the first of a series of damaging rows with the Villa hierarchy that would end in his departure from Villa Park.

The problems arose when he was called into the club's offices to sign for the following season: 'I was quite ready to sign again. But a surprise was in store for me. I went to the Aston club on the distinct understanding that I should continue to reside in Sheffield.'[1]

According to Barson, the club now insisted that if he was to continue playing for Villa he would have to move to Birmingham. Barson said he had no intentions of doing so. The arrangement whereby he lived in Sheffield, trained at Rotherham and travelled to Birmingham for matches 'had worked satisfactorily', he claimed. The fact that the 'arrangement' had almost resulted in a small catastrophe during the preceding season's FA Cup, Barson preferred to consider as nothing more than an amusing episode. Not so the Aston Villa board, which had thus decided that all their players should reside 'within a short distance of the ground' and were prepared to find houses for players who needed them.

Apparently, it had always been stipulated that Villa players should live in Birmingham but due to the shortage of housing immediately after the Great War, they had relaxed their rules. The *Nottingham Evening Post* explained: 'Although the club desired the players to live at Birmingham the Villa did not care to enforce that last season when housing difficulties were so great. This year they were most anxious that all the players should live in Birmingham and do their training under the eyes of the club officials. The Villa say that there is no reason for the men to live away now. Owing to their recent appeal they have received offers of suitable accommodation, while they are quite prepared to purchase houses for the men if need be.'[2]

There were other reasons, of course, in the immediate post-war years when industrial strikes were rife and travel inclined to be disrupted at short notice. In 1920 the *Green 'Un* reported:

> With the threat of a coal strike hanging over our heads the wise football clubs have long ago taken time by the forelock and have made arrangements for the necessary travelling should the blow fall. Some clubs even anticipated the Football League's injunction in the matter and made their arrangements as soon as trouble seemed likely.
>
> With the probable curtailment of trains it will be necessary, in the case of a strike, for footballers to make their journeys by charabanc or any other suitable means. If the demand for such vehicles becomes great the price will, as usual, soar so that the clubs who have already got things arranged are in a comfortable position. One club that I know of has made arrangements for the conveyance of their players to any place at any time during the season, should it not be possible to make the trip by train. For this they have paid a retaining fee. Things have come to pretty pass when such an arrangement is necessary or desirable; but it is a wise precaution

to make when industrial England is in such an unsettled state.[3]

Despite all this, Barson objected, insisting that there was nothing in his contract that stipulated such domiciliary arrangements. Villa then asked him to spend a month living in a hotel in Birmingham as part of pre-season training. Barson agreed, apparently under the impression that once the season began, he could move back to Sheffield. The Villa board, however, came to the conclusion that if he wanted to do that he would have to pay his own expenses, something they had been doing thus far.

'I was upset. The insistence on the part of the Villa directorate was beginning to irritate me.'

It was at that point that Barson and team-mate Clem Stephenson (who was also now being charged expenses for travelling to and from his home near Newcastle) decided to take drastic action. They failed to turn up for a match at Bolton against the Wanderers which Villa lost 5-0. In effect, they had gone on unofficial strike.

'I spent the afternoon in Sheffield. I went to a picture show. I was not worried. I knew that there would be a sensation. But I was not alarmed. I was convinced that this was the best way in which to show my determination about the matter.'[4]

He claimed later that he had no idea that Stephenson had also decided not to play at Bolton, which seems rather odd in the circumstances. It was headline news, however, and the *Sheffield Daily Telegraph* interviewed him. He explained:

BARSON'S ACCOUNT: FOOTBALL SENSATION

Andy Ducat, Clem Stephenson and myself are all in the same boat. Ducat has a business in London; Stephenson's wife in Newcastle teaches the violin to a large number of pupils; while I have a family here and a business too. When I fixed up this season I did so on the agreement that I could live in Sheffield and the club pay travelling expenses. That was, unfortunately, only a verbal agreement and now the club say that if I stay in Sheffield I must pay my own expenses. Stephenson and I are determined to make a stand on the matter and so we did not turn out on Saturday.

He claimed he bore no ill-will towards anyone on the board: 'the trouble is just over the expenses. This means a serious reduction in wages each week and is prohibitive.'

He insisted that he would not play again until he got a written agreement concerning who paid his fares. Rather than live in Birmingham, he would prefer to be placed on the transfer list. 'They certainly have offered me a house in Birmingham but I don't want to leave Sheffield.'[5]

Jack Cock, writing in *The Globe* at the same time, outlined the dispute from two angles:

PLAYERS AND THEIR HOMES

The business raises the question of players living outside the town in which their club is situated and shows up the tremendous powers vested in the manager of a professional club. The Villa manager could if he chose suspend these players for the remainder of the season (during which time they would receive no wages) and then refuse to put them on the transfer list next May. He has, as a matter of fact, used his strength humanely (as the fable says) by suspending them for a fortnight and requiring them to come to Birmingham to live within the next month.

Cock then outlined the situation in practical terms:

I should like, however, to explain why so many players now live miles and miles away from the headquarters of their clubs. It has only arisen since the war and the reason is this. Prior to 1914 a large

number of players owned their own houses. Since
then they have changed their clubs, but are unable
to find suitable accommodation close to the new
grounds. Owing to the comparative smallness
of their wages, they cannot afford – even if they
could get the houses – to pay a prohibitive rental,
or to leave their wives and families at home and
themselves live in lodgings. Besides, we were away
from our wives long enough during the war. Why
should we stay away now? It would be inhuman to
expect us to do so.[6]

What exactly the arrangements might have been
regarding the houses Villa said they had found for players
was not explained. One assumes the player would rent
a house, which someone like Barson might have found
difficult, given that he already had a home and extended
family in Grimesthorpe which he was not going to leave.

The two players ultimately met with directors and
club officials, among them Rinder, Devey, Howard
Spencer and secretary Ramsey. They were given a two-
week suspension from 16 to 30 September and told that
following that they would have to move to Birmingham.
It was emphasised that the suspension was for not turning
up to play – a breach of contract – not for refusing to
move to Birmingham.

'Care should be taken that the Bolton business and
the residence location should not be confused. One is a
matter of discipline, the other a question of principle.'

They were, however, given a month's time to arrange
for coming to live in Birmingham.

'Asked if the club would insist on both players coming to live in B/Ham Mr Ramsey said, "It looks like it, does it not?" Andy Ducat, Ramsey insisted, "had not been guilty of any act of disobedience."'[7]

It was widely reported that Barson had apologised to the board, but he later insisted he had done no such thing. What's more, 'I did not lift a finger towards getting a house in Birmingham but I made my mind up that I would continue to give my best services on the field. I know I was never more determined about anything ...'[8]

And there the matter rested. The two turned up for duty on 2 October for a match against Oldham which Villa won 3-0 and the season carried on. There was, however, according to Barson, 'a fly in the ointment but it was a small fly – a much bigger fly was hovering around'.

The argument between Barson and the Villa directors as to where he ought to live would never be satisfactorily settled. 'The position just now is that both Aston Villa's officials and Barson are "lying low" until the end of the season.'[9]

Barson carried on as normal and appeared to be happy enough on the surface, but he was, despite the on-field bravado and bluster, an insecure individual and certainly not unaware of the criticism he was now receiving on a regular basis from fans up and down the country.

'I was often finding myself very severely criticised for rough play. At various grounds I was barracked. I am fairly thick-skinned but I have a heart! And there were occasions when I used to feel disheartened because I was severely marked by my opponents. Some of them didn't show much mercy, whereupon the crowds would laugh and shout "Poor old Barson – he's getting what he deserves today!" But if poor old Barson remonstrated or gave his enemy a good honest charge – oh the howls!'[10]

He even went as far as issuing a public declaration in which he defended his approach: 'Good honest charging is a principle of the game. Without it I should not be of much use to my side. I charge while some others I know ankle-tap. Of the two I prefer the Yorkshire way. To bowl a man over by means of a shoulder-to-shoulder charge is good honest football.'[11]

His team-mates considered him invaluable, however. Billy Walker wrote in *Thomson's Weekly News*:

> I will not have it thought that he [Barson] is an out and out rough player, merely for the sake of being rough. In a charge, the weaker goes under. It doesn't happen to be Barson, that's all. He is the highwayman of soccer. You have to stand and deliver. Tis better not to stand at all. Far better get rid of the ball before he has a chance of taking it from you.[12]

Barson was certainly appreciated by football commentators, however, who could see beyond the physicality. In November 1920, for instance, one of his early mentors, Tom Boyle, wrote about the importance of the half-back line in contemporary play:

> The half-back line is the most important part of the team ... To put it in another way, the best forwards in the world won't get goals and won't

even be able make the opportunities for scoring goals unless they have the proper sort of backing from the men behind them. Equally, the best pair of backs any side can put on the field won't prove good enough for the task of holding five forwards if those forwards are simply threading their way past the half-backs time after time.

In Boyle's opinion, there were three sets of men whom he rated the very best: those of league champions West Bromwich Albion, Tottenham Hotspur and Aston Villa:

> The secret of Spurs success [is] to be found in the fact that in Smith, Rance and Grimsdell they have a half-back line which simply dominates the play in match after match. At the present time there can be doubt that Grimsdell is, as a half-back, is in a class by himself, and lucky the wing pair which has a player of his stamp behind them. They just have to play.

Furthermore,

> An instance of what a half-back line can do for a team is to be found in the experience of Aston Villa last season. In Ducat, Barson and Harrop they had three men who are all in the top class, men who can stop the other fellows from working out their schemes, and who can also play their part to help their own attackers to get with the good work of scoring goals.[13]

Interestingly, it would be the clash between the half-back lines of Spurs and Villa in the FA Cup that would define the 1920/21 season for Barson's men.

In fact, it would be the tight defensive unit that Barson organised and oversaw during the next couple of years that provided the springboard for the dashing Billy Walker to plunder so many of his early career goals.

Three Tommys – Weston, Smart and Ball – would share full-back duties, while Barson, Moss, Harrop and the stylish Andy Ducat formed a dominating half-back line.

Walker, prompted by Clem Stephenson and feeding off crosses from Kirton, Wallace, York and Dorrell, scored 31 goals in 42 games in season 1920/21. The following season, Ernest Blackburn would be added at full-back, George Blackburn at left-half when Ducat moved on to Fulham, while Ian Dickson, with 28 goals in 42 games, supported Kirton (13 goals) and the irrepressible Walker (33 goals) up front as York and Dorrell raided down the wings.

Billy Walker would be the star, of course; young, dashing and destined to become a Villa 'legend', he would earn 18 England caps over a 15-year period and score over 200 goals for Villa in almost 500 appearances (which makes him Villa's all-time top scorer to this day).

Barson's influence on Walker was immense. Years later, Walker claimed he could still hear Barson yelling 'Hit it' from behind him, 'and know that as I hit it I could almost depend on hearing "Good lad" in the same bellow'.

'Once or twice I came unstuck. I remember one time I was about midfield on our side of the centre line and the ball came to me. Just before it reached me I heard the "Hit it!" I met it full on and by the greatest fluke in the world the ball soared towards the other goal and dipped under the bar. While everybody was yelling about Walker's wonder goal, Frank Barson ran past me and gave me a nudge that almost cracked three ribs.

'Although I knew it was a fluke, I still thought the goal deserved better treatment than that, and I looked at him in pained surprise.

'"I said, Hit it!" he said and I couldn't help but say, "Well, I did didn't I?"

'He glared at me and said darkly, "I meant to the right, young 'un, you should have known that."

'With a man like Barson, you learned from almost every ball.'[14]

In the league the Villa began season 1920/21 well enough with a crushing 5-0 win over Arsenal at Villa Park, where 47,000 saw Walker score four goals in brilliant fashion, but it would be in the cup that, once again, the thrills and spills would occur.

Villa defeated Bristol City in the first round and followed that with a tough encounter with Notts County. Following a 0-0 draw at the County ground in front of 50,000 spectators which saw, 'Rough play in the ascendancy'[15] and the referee having to administer a general caution to the whole of the players, a Billy Walker goal saw Villa through in the replay. Notts County would ultimately come again.

In the next round, Villa met their cup final opponents of the previous year, Huddersfield Town, and in front of 60,627 (earning receipts of £3,017) they achieved a convincing two-goal victory that installed them as favourites once again for the cup.

Huddersfield made a disastrous start to the game, conceding two goals within the first four minutes, the opening goal coming from a free kick for a foul on Kirton just outside the penalty area. Walker took it and his rising shot flew straight into the corner of the net, 'causing Bullock and keeper Mutch to look with astonishment at each other'. Walker then scored a second with a fine hooked shot and Huddersfield never recovered.

In early March, it was Tottenham Hotspur once again before a crowd of 51,991, only this time it would be Spurs who scored the only goal. 'Observer' wrote: '[Spurs] played beautiful football at a great pace, which made the holders look quite a moderate side. As a matter of fact, the Villa played well, and, for a time, their admirable half-backs checked the home forwards just the same way as the Tottenham middle line prevented the Villa forwards from doing any effective work. For nearly 20 minutes neither goalkeeper had a shot to save, and almost the first really good attempt at goal proved effective. Banks, playing outside-right, worked into the inside position to receive a pass from Dimmock, and he placed his shot so that Hardy had no chance of getting to the ball.'[16]

Thereafter, the play was largely in the Villa half, with Spurs thoroughly deserving their fine success over the holders.

Jimmy Catton in *Athletic News* commented:

> Barson as ever went through the game more like a steam engine than a man.[17]

In the league, however, Villa failed to maintain their fine form of the autumn and would finish tenth with 43 points, one of their last matches being a 5-1 thrashing by Chelsea, during which Barson conceded and then won a penalty while his old foe Jack Cock ran riot, scoring a hat-trick. Cock had clearly learned from his earlier painful experience in the FA Cup. As Barson noted, 'Every dog has his day.' Sadly for Villa, their Barson days were rapidly running out.

Endnotes
1. Mems
2. *Nottingham Evening Post*, 21 September 1920
3. *Green 'Un*, 2 October 1920
4. Mems
5. *Sheffield Daily Telegraph*, 21 September 1920
6. *The Globe*, 25 September 1920
7. *Birmingham Daily Gazette*, 28 September 1920
8. Mems
9. *Sheffield Daily Telegraph*, 24 September 1920
10. Mems
11. Ditto
12. *Thomson's Weekly News*, 1925
13. *Derbyshire Advertiser and Journal*, 26 November 1920
14. Billy Walker, *Soccer in the Blood* (London: Stanley Paul, 1960)
15. *Sheffield Daily Telegraph*, 18 January 1921
16. *Exeter and Plymouth Gazette*, 7 March 1921
17. *Athletic News*, 7 March 1921

Chapter Eleven

Fires Slumbering Beneath

'He is still living in Sheffield and training at Rotherham, but, though the Villa have endeavoured to pacify him, fires slumber beneath ...' **Sheffield Daily Telegraph, Tuesday, 18 January 1921.**

'Now Barson urges that he has a business in the Sheffield area. There are other conditions which Batson is understood to insist upon, and the Villa feel that they ought not to give way.' **Athletic News, Monday, 23 May 1921.**

IN AUGUST 1921, *Athletic News* reported:

Barson Quite Happy. Barson has settled down quite comfortably with Aston Villa, and is throwing himself heart and soul into the work of the club. Barson is a wholehearted player and abhors friction. Still living in Sheffield, Barson is staying in Birmingham until the opening of the football season in order that he may be constantly in attendance at Villa Park. As a matter of fact, Barson normally trains with Rotherham, and one may say that he has now a definite agreement with the Villa in which all that he may do and may not do is set down. Barson speaks with some enthusiasm about the promise of the young talent Aston Villa have.[1]

Whatever the agreement was as to what he 'may or may not do', Barson still appeared uneasy. 'I was of the solid opinion that the club were going back upon a promise made to me earlier on,' he would write. However, financial terms with the club appeared satisfactory and Barson was once again leading the team. In fact, he'd been appointed captain.

During the close season, though, many of his close friends on the playing staff had left. First, Clem Stephenson was lured away to Huddersfield by Herbert Chapman, who would build one of his first new title-winning sides around the veteran inside-forward. Then Andy Ducat joined Fulham, followed by the departures of long-serving forward Harrop and keeper Sam Hardy.

In the league, Villa were far too inconsistent, losing 15 away games, although finishing fifth in the table as Liverpool became champions. More had been hoped for, especially as for almost two-thirds of the season they had been considered title contenders.

Along the way, Barson proved himself a fine captain and leader, a good example being a December match against Sheffield United in which he scored what he considered to be his finest goal – and one that some supporters were still talking about 40 years later!

Having established a two-goal lead, Villa were then pegged back and it was Barson who organised the resistance:

> What took the gilt off the play was the decision of the Villa captain to hold up the home attacks by playing one back for the greater part of the match. In fairness, I do not think he could be blamed, for it was United who started the practice. However, the Villa kept Blackburn among the half-backs obstinately and mercilessly, till the crowd was heartily sick of the sound of the harassed referee's whistle, and the sight of attacks broken off short at promising stages. One desperate individual with a large voice reminded Barson, the Villa captain, that he is a Sheffielder himself, and many besought him to 'play the game'. But Barson was determined that his lesson should be driven home.[2]

Despite this, United scored twice to draw level. Barson then took matters into his own hands – or rather head:

> It was about seven minutes from the end and a draw seemed assured, but Villa rallied, and after a thrilling burst on the right York forced a corner. The players lined up for the kick, Barson, for once,

being well out of the ruck, but that was the strategy.
York framed for the kick, hesitated, and, just as the
captain clapped his hands, finally let drive and as
true as an arrow the ball shot straight from Barson's
head, and the game was over.[3]

In fact, the ball flew past Gough so fast that many people
thought Barson had kicked it.

As it was, it would be the FA Cup that once again
provided the real drama for Villa fans that season, not
all of it to their liking. Villa began their campaign in
brilliant fashion by thrashing Derby County 6-1, a
Walker hat-trick putting them 5-0 up at half-time.

Two weeks later, however, disaster struck. In a league
match (actually Villa's 1,000th in league competition)
against Everton at Goodison Park, Villa lost a 1-0 lead
(and ultimately the match) as Bobby Irvine scored a
sensational five-minute hat-trick.

As Irvine completed his hat-trick, however, there
came what the *Birmingham Daily Gazette*'s 'Touchstone'
described as 'A Breezy Incident'.

> Barson, too late to check his ride to the rescue,
> collided with the centre-forward and the pair rolled
> into the mud under the net. Irvine, in a wildly
> excited manner, turned over as he lay and punched
> Barson – and Crossley and Fazackerley who had
> by that time also reached the net, joined in the
> excitement.
>
> The consequence was a situation closely
> resembling a common brawl in which other

players appeared likely to become involved. Indeed, Jackson received a stray bump or two, while Killen and York, running in to make peace, did not escape scathless.

Referee Kirby, meantime, had been all unconscious of the affair, walking up towards the centre ready for the resumption of play, but the linesmen and one of the trainers had gone to the playing area to render assistance. Crossley went away rubbing his chin very gingerly, and Irvine

and Jackson looked none too happy, otherwise no
damage was done, and there was never any further
suggestion of bad feeling.[4]

The 'bad feeling', however, was to occur after the match
but not between the players. According to Barson, a Villa
director seated in the Villa dressing room after the match
caused the trouble.

As the Villa players were changing, Everton's
Stan Fazackerley entered – not to continue the earlier
fistfight but to wait for Barson as the two men, along
with a couple of music-hall entertainer friends of
Fazackerley's, were intending to spend the evening
out on the town.

The Villa director objected to Fazackerley being
present and asked him to leave. Barson demurred saying
Fazackerley could stay until he, Barson, was ready. The
director insisted, however, citing the Villa rule that
barred 'strangers' from being present in the dressing
room. Barson then lost his temper:

'I looked "pug". I tell you. I let rip. I couldn't help it.
Fazackerley withdrew – very wisely. But my conscience,
I talked, I said rash things. I was really angry. I can quite
imagine that some people might say I was living up to
my reputation. I know very well that certain of my critics
regard me as a kind of football bandit, a man whose hand
is against everyone and that everyone's hand is against
me. Well, such views have not worried me. There is no
doubt that I put over the "bandit" spirit this time. Some
of my club mates called out – "Steady Frank – it's no use
talking like that."'

At this point Villa chairman Rinder appeared but Barson continued ranting, using, in his words, 'un-Parliamentary language'.

'The directors appealed to me to control myself. It seemed impossible ... nothing could bring me round to what was asked for – "a sensible view".'

Barson had lost control and he acknowledged it: 'I was terribly embittered. I just felt that I never wanted to kick another football for Aston Villa.'

He later admitted, 'I was perfectly aware of the fact that the Villa directorate objected to strangers coming into our dressing room ... but while the Villa rules were usually strict and whilst certain disciplinary measures irritated now and then, it never entered my head for a single moment that I was acting foolishly in extending an invitation to Fazackerley, a very gentlemanly fellow, a worthy opponent, particularly so on this fatal day and, what was more, a personal friend and a frequent travelling companion.'[5]

Fazackerley may well have been a 'very gentlemanly fellow' but he was also something of a loose cannon, whose own career would be punctuated by clashes with authority. What's more, in later accounts of the incident, Barson omitted the context – the earlier brawl during the Villa–Everton match just finished that had involved Fazackerley, the fact that it had marred a special occasion – the 1,000th Villa match – not to mention the fact that Villa had lost in surprising fashion.

There was a later suggestion that the argument concerning Fazackerley was because of fears that the earlier on-field clash might be repeated, but Barson had made the situation clear enough. Intriguingly, it was much later revealed that an earlier incident had occurred in the dressing room that might well have added to the tension in the air. Frank Moss recalled, 'Everton's left-half Grenyer was having his benefit so before the game he came into our dressing room and put two bottles of sherry onto the table for us to drink after the match. In those days the directors never came into the dressing room before or after the match – yet before this Everton battle one of the Villa board came and sat down in our room. "If he thinks he's going to have a tot, he's going to be unlucky," Frank said in a loud voice with a nod towards the sherry.'[6]

Whatever the fine detail, the upshot was inevitable: Barson was suspended by the club and asked to apologise for his outburst as well as for the breach in regulations. It was headline news again, not the sort of publicity that Villa welcomed.

Barson once again stated that he'd not apologised: 'I could not get it out of my head that a friend had been slighted when there was no particular need for it.' He added, however, that the argument was not the reason why he subsequently decided to leave Villa. 'I would not say that the scene in the dressing room and its sequel were responsible for this decision and I would not say that it was the residence question …'[7]

The reason could well have been that Barson was growing irked by the nature of the Villa 'regime' and its paternalistic attitude towards players. The Star *Green 'Un* reported in 1922:

(A VILLA SECRET

We have heard many stories of how Aston Villa
build up winning teams. The latest that they keep
their players on the ground on training days, and
have lunch together. It is also said to be a fact that
the players have blackboard football lessons with
Howard Spencer often lecturer.)[8]

Quite obviously, players during the interwar period had
far less freedom than modern players. What's more,
they were inclined to put up with being ordered about
in ways that today would simply not be tolerated. The
Villa chairman, Rinder, was noted for his disciplinarian
tendencies. He was, as Billy Walker called him,
a 'martinet'.

The tales told of how players tended to respond
to Rinder gave a flavour of the atmosphere. Walker
recounted the following incident concerning full-back
Tommy Smart: 'It was one of Villa's "inflexible rules":
all players must be at the station 20 minutes before the
departure of the train. On this occasion Tommy Smart
arrived two minutes before the train was due to leave,
panting and out of breath having run all the way from
Snow Hill station. As he went to board the train, Rinder
asked him, "What time is this, Smart?"

'"Just in time to catch the train," Smart answered.
Rinder wasn't amused.

'"You had better go back to Villa Park and tell them
you are playing in the reserves tomorrow," he ordered.

'"I've been picked to play at Newcastle and it's to
Newcastle I am going," Smart responded.

"'Go back instantly to Villa Park and do as you are told,'" Rinder thundered.

"'Not likely,'" Smart replied. "'I'm going to Newcastle and you can please thissen.'" He then pushed past the chairman who didn't know what to say or do. Smart played, and the team won. After the match, Rinder approached him and said, "Well played, Smart, you were wonderful. I'll now try and forget what happened yesterday.'"[9]

Walker told the tale to illustrate Smart's 'personality' but it says a lot more about Rinder than Smart. There was also the petty snobbery that players had to endure.

Barson recalled that on one occasion he and Frank Moss needed a drink after a training session so they popped into a nearby pub. 'We were busy downing a pint when in walked the Villa secretary George Ramsey and all the office staff. Nothing was said at the time but that afternoon Mr Ramsey sent for me and told me that as the office staff had their lunch at the pub every day I would have to have my drink elsewhere in future. It was the first and only time I'd had a drink like that but it didn't stop me telling him that if anyone was going to change pubs – it was him!'[10]

Fred Archer, the ex-Aston Villa secretary, recalled another petty incident, this time involving Barson and the club manager George Ramsey: 'I had been sent to get Frank from the dressing rooms in the Witton Lane Stand and on his way back to Mr Ramsey's office our centre-half had walked straight across the pitch. In those days this was an unforgiveable crime. No one, apart from the groundsman, was allowed on the pitch and Mr Ramsey gave him a quick telling off. Barson's reply was typical. "You don't allow me to walk across the pitch in ordinary shoes but on match days I can run all over the f… place in my football boots!" Archer added that he would never have dreamt of walking on the pitch. 'That Barson incident is something I'll never forget.'[11]

When grown men can recall such moments almost 50 years later, it says a lot about the social situation of players in general. Unlike many of his more phlegmatic colleagues, Barson tended to find such treatment infuriating.

With Barson suspended, Villa scraped through the next round of the FA Cup by the only goal against Third Division Luton Town. In the third round, Stoke held Villa to a goalless draw on their own ground but were put out 4-0 at Villa Park. Then came a home draw against Notts County, once formidable rivals but now a lowly Second Division side.

Villa drew 2-2 at Meadow Lane and there seemed little doubt about the outcome of the replay on the following Wednesday at Villa Park. However, the County put up a terrific and totally unexpected fight. Although Villa were twice in the lead, Notts equalised five minutes from the end of normal time and scored a shock winner during the extra half-hour.

The final goal was a contentious one, with Villa appealing for offside. As J.T. Howcroft was the referee, however, Barson might not have been to the fore in that respect. He would certainly not have liked the *Daily Sketch*'s summary of Notts' victory either: 'Notts tackled the Villa almost in the fashion of a terrier dealing with a rat. They gripped them, shook them and finally completely mastered them.'

Albert Iremonger, the thin and angular County goalkeeper and a great character of the period, gave magnificent displays in both games. It's said that the Aston fans never forgave him. In fact, some three years later, when County were league visitors, Albert, who again thwarted the Villa forwards, was bombarded with oranges.

Villa's season would finally end with a dispiriting 3-1 defeat at the hands of lowly Oldham Athletic, who'd finished two places above relegation. It would be the last game Barson played for Aston Villa.

'Towards the end of that season I made up my mind quite definitely that I would not care to remain with the Villa much longer. But the Villa did not want to finish with me. The club offered me good terms. I would not accept them. I lost my summer wages. I could not get rid of a strained feeling towards the club.'[12]

The cynic might suggest that Barson's decision to leave the club was motivated less by his finer feelings and more by the opportunity to make some money. The cynic would be correct, although there was more to the story than simple avarice.

Barson was now 31 years old but still at the height of his powers as a player. He was clearly sought-after: Sheffield United had made enquiries earlier in the season and during the close season Burnley tried to talk him into signing for them. Villa could expect a large fee if they sold him and, under the rules then governing the game, Barson might well be in line for a share, a percentage, of the money paid, which he'd missed when leaving Barnsley. There was, however, a wider issue involved.

In the 1960s, Barson revealed that the Football League's decision in 1922 to cut players' wages from £9 to £8 (and to peremptorily alter existing players' contracts into the bargain) played a big part in his decision to leave Villa.

The massive increases in football attendances that had occurred so suddenly after 1919 had by now gone into reverse and caught the football industry by surprise. Expensive extensions and ground improvements found clubs running into debt and facing losses ranging from hundreds to many thousands of pounds, particularly those situated in areas hard hit by the post-war trade recession: Durham City registered a loss in 1922 of almost £2,000, Grimsby of £3,000, and Bristol City approaching £4,000.

Nevertheless, the unilateral decision to cut players' wages, taken in April 1922 at an emergency meeting of the League Management Committee, came as a bolt out of the blue. The Players' Union, at that point a relatively weak body with few resources, considered calling a strike but feared nothing would come of it.

Instead, it mounted a risky court case to question the legality of the league's decision. Union solicitor Hinchcliffe felt that the League, in altering rule seven to introduce a new maximum wage, had forced clubs into breaching a number of contracts. As secretary Harry Newbould said in a letter to *Athletic News*:

> It is common knowledge that this rule was practically forced on the clubs, that they had no

opportunity to consider it and that many of them voted for it only under strong pressure and with great reluctance. It is also common knowledge that the rule was introduced on the eve of signing-on time. In other words it was a pistol levelled at the players' heads without reasonable consideration by the clubs or players.[13]

The Union financed the case of Henry Leddy, a Dubliner, centre-half and captain of Chesterfield, who had previously played for Tranmere Rovers and Everton in the First Division. Leddy had signed his contract in March 1922, guaranteeing him £9 a week all year round until May 1923. The League resolution had come a month later, and Leddy had refused to sign a new contract. He had, it was announced, 'brought his action to contest the right of the club or the Football League to break his existing contract under the common law of the land'.

On 8 May 1923 at the Royal Court of Justice in the Strand, Mr Justice Lush and Mr Justice Salter allowed the Union's appeal and awarded Leddy his back pay and costs for both hearings. The League declined to take the matter further and abandoned the action. Leddy, and the Players' Union, had won a small but significant victory.

By then, Barson had taken matters into his own hands. He recalled: 'The Players' Union instructed players NOT to re-sign unless they were given the extra pound. The strike was doomed to failure. As it was during the close season football was not affected and few players had been receiving £9 anyway. Gradually the players began to sneak back to re-sign. The strike, which never really began, was over except for one man … Frank Barson! I made up my mind to leave Villa so I re-fused to re-sign until I was transferred to Manchester United.'[14]

United's terms may well have been superior to those Villa were offering. At the very least, however, Barson felt it was his last opportunity to obtain that precious transfer fee percentage, as in the ensuing years his worth on the market would obviously decline. Sadly for Barson, things would not work out as planned.

Villa at first refused to let him go. 'The club offered me good terms. I would not accept them. I lost my summer wages.'

Villa held out until the very last, however, finally relenting when Barson declared, 'You might just as well pocket the big transfer fee you will receive. If you don't let me kick a ball for another club I'll never kick a ball for you again.'

He finally signed for Manchester United for a fee of £5,000 in late September 1922.

W.L.U in the *Liverpool Echo* opined:

> He is a born leader. He is conscientious, too, never flagging, never giving up; perhaps he uses his splendid physical attributes too much, perhaps his robust methods are not always admired but he is essentially a vigorous, aggressive player. Tis the nature of the man. How great his loss to the Villa is time will show.[15]

Billy Walker was in no doubt as to Barson's worth. 'It is an axiom of football that one man does not make a team.

Barson is the exception that proves the rule, for most certainly his tremendous command of the field made the great Aston Villa side, of which I was a young and very proud member. I am unhesitating in saying that he was the greatest captain of them all. And I don't want to rub in the point too far. His presence on the field was worth all the tactical talks of a dozen coaches off it.'[16]

Endnotes
1. *Athletic News*, 15 August 1921
2. *Sheffield Daily Telegraph*, 27 December 1921
3. *Birmingham Daily Gazette*, 27 December 1921
4. *Birmingham Daily Gazette*, 23 January 1922
5. Mems
6. *Sports Argus*, 15 April 1961
7. Mems
8. *Star Green 'Un*, 11 March 1922
9. Billy Walker, *Soccer in the Blood* (London: Stanley Paul, 1960)
10. Mems, 1960
11. *Sports Argus*, 31 May 1969
12. Mems
13. John Harding, *Behind The Glory: 100 Years of the PFA* (Breedon Books Publishing Company, 2009)
14. The Frank Barson Story, *Sports Argust*, 27 August 1960
15. *Liverpool Football Echo*, 2 September 1922
16. Billy Walker, *Soccer in the Blood* (London: Stanley Paul, 1960), p.92

Chapter Twelve

Bouncing Off Barson

'All eyes were naturally on Barson but the ex-Villa man was not particularly noticeable, though his influence was undoubtedly felt. With those crafty forward passes of his he was often effective, though the forwards might have used them better. Again, in racing back to thwart a dangerous raid and in having a finger in the winning goal he was more than useful so that Manchester could be more than satisfied.' **Birmingham Daily Gazette, Monday, 11 September 1922.**

'If you throw a rubber ball against a wall it will bounce off and lightweights bounce off a player of the build of Barson' **Manchester Football News, The Right Spirit, April 1923.**

BARSON'S MOVE to Manchester United in late 1922 was not the shock that his transfer from Barnsley to Villa had been three seasons before but was still something of a surprise to some observers. During the summer a number of First Division clubs, including Burnley, Everton and Oldham Athletic, had made serious enquiries after Barson once Villa had given him permission to speak to various suitors. Burnley, in particular, made strenuous efforts. Football League runners-up in 1920, champions in 1922, they were one of the top sides in the early 1920s. Their manager Jack Haworth met Barson at a hotel in Manchester and did his best, but Barson refused Burnley's offer: 'I can't really say why except that I do not and never did like Burnley, although I have many friends there ...'

Manchester United was no longer considered one of the league's premier clubs; in fact, they had just been relegated to the Second Division. They had made enquiries for Barson at the end of the 1922 season but Aston Villa were then asking a prohibitive £6,000 – which would have been another transfer record. As the close season ended, however, and Villa's efforts to persuade Barson to stay began to look hopeless, they relented and dropped the price to £5,000, still a considerable sum.

Barson suggests in his memoirs that there were certain 'conditions' that needed meeting before he signed: that he should be allowed to live in Sheffield, of course; the level of his weekly wage; plus a promised lump sum, 'equivalent to his share of benefit under ordinary circumstance.' The problem with the latter was that the club might *offer* to pay the money, which Villa did, but it needed to be sanctioned by the Football League.

The specific rule read: 'When a player is transferred, the club transferring him may, *with the consent of the Management Committee*, as a reward for loyal and meritorious service, pay such player in lieu of presumed accrued share of benefit, a percentage ...'

Barson was in no doubt he qualified. 'I told the committee very plainly that I considered I had served Villa well and that the money paid by the Villa to Barnsley had been repaid with interest.'[1]

He was in for a nasty surprise, however. After two meetings of the League Management Committee they decided he didn't qualify, largely because he had, in their words, 'forced the hand of his club to transfer him'.

Barson was left bemused and hurt. Other players had received such sums after actually *breaking* their contracts. Barson had simply refused to sign a new one and had also forfeited at least three/four months' wages in the process.

In many ways it was a mystery as to why Villa had suggested he would receive the money in the first place when they should have known that it would be refused. (Even more curious, before he signed for Manchester United, the club had approached the League for permission to pay Barson the back wages he'd lost by not signing a new contract.)

The League, in fact, punished Villa for what it considered a waste of everyone's time by insisting the club pay the enquiries expenses. At least Barson was spared that indignity. (He wasn't alone in being refused such a percentage – his old pal Stan Fazackerley also suffered in such a way.)

Barson's famous opponents

'Of course I had to bow my knee to the Management Committee but outside the Euston Hotel in London where the decision was announced I felt sorely depressed on leaving for my home. Had I forced the hands of Aston Villa? In a sense I had done so ... It was true that I wanted to leave Aston Villa. But what of that? We were not slaves. Or at least we ought not to be, I said ... I was disappointed, bitterly. It meant a loss to me of several hundreds of pounds ...' (£700 was the amount he might have got, equal to £40,000 today.)

'I do not like nursing grievances. They give your system a sort of jaundice effect. But it is rather difficult to forget this financial disappointment!'[2]

In fact, he may well have found his thoughts turning back to grandmother Mary Ann and her rebuttal at the hands of other men in authority. There would be one silver lining, however, albeit a distant one. As part of the inducement to sign for the Old Trafford club, a director and prominent brewer, John Henry Davies, appears to have promised Barson the tenancy of his own public house if the club gained promotion to the top flight within three years of Frank's signing. It was something of an about turn, however, when he'd refused to move to Villa for three years – although that dispute had been largely about money and expenses.

Nevertheless, apart from the (false) prospect of money, one wonders what it was about Manchester United that attracted him. Their glory days of the pre-First World War era were long gone, their last title won back in 1911. Their talismanic leader, the Welsh Wizard Billy Meredith, had finally quit the club over a wages dispute in July 1921 – and had gone across town to Manchester City for a final swansong. What's more, their manager, John Chapman, the man who had presumably persuaded Barson to sign for the club, was an unknown figure in English football.

Chapman wasn't quite the dour, colourless character portrayed by some contemporary writers, however. He possessed a temper and had been known to berate referees in colourful language in his playing days in Scotland. As manager of Airdrieonians, he'd been reasonably successful, winning Scottish cups and establishing the club as a second-tier force behind the ever-dominant Celtic/Rangers duo. His best signing for Airdrie had been the young Hughie Gallagher, who would go on to achieve fame with Newcastle United and Scotland.

Chapman had been lured south in October 1921 to assist the ailing United manager John Robson, who passed away in January 1922. Offered a five-year contract, a house and a four-figure salary, plus a sizeable transfer budget, Chapman was given the task of revitalising the team who were then lying 19th in the First Division. He tried the usual 'bonding' techniques in order to foster a sense of 'family': players eating together and indulging in playing card evenings and smoking concerts. On the playing front he bought a talented midfielder, Neil McBain, from Ayr United for £4,500 plus David Ellis and Willie Henderson from Airdrie for £3,000, but the results did not improve and the club was relegated in April 1922.

Thus, when Barson walked into the Old Trafford dressing room in September 1922 he found himself amid a group of reasonably talented but leaderless players, a collection of long-serving professionals and raw youth, some time-servers plus one or two expensive failures. There were no players to match the likes of Sam Hardy, Andy Ducat, Billy Kirton and Clem Stephenson – certainly no one approaching the peerless skills of Barson's protégé, the free-scoring Billy Walker.

There was Jack Mew, a safe keeper and an excellent handler of the ball, who would play over 500 games for the club and be succeeded by Alf Steward, who would be on United's books for 11 years and 300+ appearances.

There were two full-backs (described by club historian Dr Percy Young as 'two of the greatest full-backs ever to play for United'): Jack Silcock, a classy player from nearby Eccles who would make 400+ appearances for United and earn three England caps, usually alongside Charlie Moore, another safe and sound player (300+ games for United). They would initially share duties with Charlie Radford until the latter's untimely death.

Barson's half-back partners would normally include Clarence 'Clarry' Hilditch, a one-club man who would amass over 300 club appearances; veteran Frank Mann, already in his 30s when joining United from Huddersfield, who could also play at inside-forward, and John Grimwood, who would clock up almost 200 appearances for United.

Up front, there was Joe Spence, who played in over 500 Manchester United games, scoring 158 goals, and who would be the club's top scorer on seven occasions; Scotsman Arthur Lochhead, an inside-forward who would average a goal every three games; Frank McPherson at outside-left and Ted Partridge on the left wing.

The defence, it was claimed, was solid enough (although the stats hardly prove it. During their relegation year, they conceded 73, letting in three goals or more on 12 separate occasions). At the other end, the forwards simply could not score enough goals (41 in 42 matches). As one of the team commented, 'When we were a goal down we knew we had had it.'

Scoring goals in league football was becoming a problem in general, however. Syrian, writing in the *Daily Herald* in August 1923, opined:

> In England, almost without exception, the premier clubs sacrifice everything to the fetish of speed. Ball control, shooting skill, passing genius, all count of little value compared with speed. This hankering after speed is the bugbear of English football. Evidence of this – no League team last year was able to average two goals a match. A small task to do really, but the presumably highly skilled, and certainly highly paid, forwards failed to do it. It's a terrible admission really, but every club manager throughout England is making it – he wants a real live centre-forward. Will this season produce one?[3]

Manchester United certainly hadn't found such a player and wouldn't for some years to come. But that was probably the decisive point for Barson: Manchester United was nothing if not a challenge. He liked nothing better than a battle against the odds and found nothing more exhilarating than to step into a failing dressing room and galvanise a group of doubting players, to enthuse them with the old 'Barnsley Punch'. It also seemed that Barson felt more at home in a lower division, striving to reach upwards. Barnsley had always been his spiritual home: Barson was something of an expert at tilting at windmills.

Barson summed up his approach in an article he penned for the *Biggleswade Chronicle* a year after arriving at Old Trafford. How is it, he asked, that 'better teams' are regularly defeated by 'lesser' teams, especially in the FA Cup?

'We have seen, in the old days, clubs like the one with which I was first connected – Barnsley – win the trophy, although at the time they did this they were merely a very ordinary side in the Second Division of the league. In winning the cup, Barnsley had to remove from the competition several teams from the First Division, and we may rightly assume that by a certain measure some of these teams were better than the Barnsley side. How did it happen?'

He conceded that on occasions bad luck played its part: 'although as a footballer I must confess that we are apt, as a class, to blame our ill-fortune when we could very properly blame our bad football. That is a tendency which should be curbed as much as possible.

'How is this done? Well, in the first place, it often done by the right sort of tactics; by employing such methods that the clever footballers are put completely off their game, and thus they become, for the time being, the inferior side from a match-winning point of view.

'Again, convinced that the weaker sides, in the footballing sense, often triumph in the cup competition by sheer force of energy, which is the same as saying that they get themselves into absolutely the tip-top of condition, and with each player doing the work of two men, the poorer side, in the footballing sense, come through on top by sheer hard work.'[4]

Sadly for Barson, his giant-killing days in the FA Cup would not come again. In the ensuing three-year struggle to escape from the Second Division, his Manchester United team – now the underdogs, of course – would be eliminated early on by dominant First Division opponents.

In 1923 Tottenham Hotspur would 'trounce' United 4-0; in 1924 Huddersfield Town would 'destroy' United 3-0 in front of 66,000 at Old Trafford; and in 1925 it would be Second Division Sheffield Wednesday's turn to turf United out in the first round at Hillsborough 2-0.

Only after they had reached the First Division, in 1926, would United manage to reach an FA Cup semi-final – and they wouldn't reach another one for the next 22 years ...

Barson's 'sheer hard work' in the ensuing seasons would be dedicated to dragging a mediocre side up and out of the Second Division and then striving to keep them in the First Division, and it's no exaggeration to say that he almost did it single-handedly and at some physical cost to himself.

The Barson effect was in scant evidence early on in his first season. United won six of their first eight games, although the man himself missed the first four of those due to lack of fitness. He belatedly made his debut in a victory over Wolverhampton Wanderers at Molineux, the first of two 1-0 wins against Wolves within the space of a week in mid-September. Unfortunately, they wouldn't win another match until the beginning of December, by which time a certain amount of dissention had started to creep into the camp.

The mood around the club wasn't helped by a serious accident that occurred outside the Old Trafford ground involving United's promising young winger Willie Sarvis, who was run over by a motorcar as he was about to join a charabanc taking the reserves to Bury. The local MP, Sir Edwin Stockton, who eventually paid Sarvis some £400 in compensation, was driving the car and it would take Sarvis a year to recover – he'd eventually move to Bradford City.

On the pitch, things were not going to plan. In the *Derby Daily Telegraph*'s Football Gossip column it was noted:

BARSON NOT A SUCCESS

Frank Barson is not playing the football at Old Trafford that he did when with the Villa, and is believed that his style of play does not fit with that of his colleagues. But a cynic says that Barson is such a great player that Manchester should get players whose style fits in with his, and not expect Barson to come down to the level of his mates.[5]

Match reports, however, suggest that Barson was already 'a warm favourite with supporters with his neat and clever football and general-ship', and his power in the tackle,

Frank Barson
(Manchester United).

Barson's famous nose

not to mention his tendency to retaliate when a team-mate was fouled.

Against Clapton Orient in November, 'The big United centre-half made Herculean efforts to get something out of an overpowered set of forwards, and he himself made the best shot of the match from a free kick, A. Wood – son of Harry Wood, the one-time famous Wolf – getting down a fast, long-driven ball very well.'[6] Regularly plastered from head to foot in mud, sporting various bandages to face and leg, Barson's 'Herculean' efforts were never going to be enough to secure early promotion, however.

As one reporter put it: 'An early season penchant for snatching victory with almost the last kick of the match certainly has its exciting episodes but it does not suggest the margin of superiority necessary to maintain a lead ... they still have no ability to shoot hard and true for the net ...'[7]

By Christmas, with just three wins in the preceding 15 games, the strain began to tell on some players. Neil McBain, the expensive Chapman purchase of a season earlier, had already agreed to move from centre-half to wing-half to accommodate the arrival of Barson. As problems mounted up front, he then agreed to move forward to inside-right, scoring twice against Rotherham and Stockport County, but results had not improved.

McBain was a skilful Scottish player, a ball player, artistic and stylish, but not suited to the hurly-burly of the English Second Division. In January he shocked the club by asking for a transfer. A number of Scottish football writers dug deeper:

Matters do not appear to have been going any too smoothly at Old Trafford, and the climax was reached on Saturday, when McBain was left out of the team. The reason given out was that he was being given 'a well-earned rest,' but it has since been stated that the true reason was that the players told the manager that if McBain was in the team they would not turn out. Consequently he was left out after having been selected.[8]

A week later, another Scottish correspondent lifted the lid on what was happening at Old Trafford:

The decision of Jock Wood, following fast on that of McBain, together with what we ourselves know from other excellent sources, proves to our satisfaction that, for some reason or other, there is a dead set against certain Scottish players with Manchester United.

Wood wishes, as Neil McBain wishes, that he had never gone to Old Trafford. 'Things are rotten here,' he writes to a friend in Glasgow. 'I am the same as Neil now, other players refuse to speak to me. I should like to get back to Scottish football.' Jock has been playing capital football this season but complains bitterly of the criticism to which he is subjected, saying that the desire seems to be to get rid of all the Scottish players.[9]

On 23 January McBain moved to Everton for £4,500, a transfer that created a great deal of indignation among

Manchester United followers and the Supporters' Club – said to be several thousand strong – held a meeting to discuss the player's departure and the events that led up to it. Mr Greenough, secretary of the Supporters' Club, declared to a big audience that a deputation, of which he was a member, waited upon the club's directors and learned the full facts of the case.

'These, he said, were that after McBain had played a good game against West Ham he played indifferently against Hull City. After the match he was chaffed in the dressing room by his fellow players, who contended that Barson, the famous English centre-half, would have made a better show.

'McBain resented the remarks, and coolness arose between him and certain other members of the team. Ultimately McBain demanded that he be transferred. The audience received this explanation without enthusiasm.'[10]

That Barson had forced McBain out of the club seems unlikely. Barson later wrote that there were no problems between himself and McBain and that they were, 'On the best of terms. I say that without the fear of contradiction. I know that I was very much surprised and annoyed to find that suggestions had been made to the effect that I was responsible for a disturbed atmosphere.'[11]

He even conceded that McBain was a versatile 'splendid player' while he, Barson, was not. He could only play in one position, whereas McBain could play forward as well.

The man who engineered McBain's transfer would sum the latter's predicament up many years later:

As an artiste, McBain could knock spots off Barson, but as a destructive pivot, Barson had Neil beaten almost to a frazzle. His positional play was almost perfect. I have watched Barson in action time and again and been fascinated by the way he made the ball find him. It was almost uncanny. Away would dash the opposing forward on a menacing move.

Where was Barson? One failed to pick him out right away. But he would be certain to come into view at the psychological moment – and in the proper place. Otherwise, Barson was a rough and unlettered half-back prone to disregard certain laws and repeatedly coming into contact with the referee ... this then was the fellow whose coming had capsized Neil's apple-cart.[12]

The paths of McBain and Barson would cross again in the near future, but for now the Scotsman's departure saw an immediate upturn in United's fortunes. They would lose just three of the remaining 19 games all season, including a 6-1 thrashing of the eventual Second Division champions Notts County, and finish a respectable fourth, just three points behind West Ham United, who went up as runner-up.

That same West Ham United would feature in the first Wembley FA Cup Final against Bolton Wanderers on the same day that Barson and his team-mates finished the season in humdrum fashion at Barnsley, Barson's old club, the two teams competing in a 'tame' 2-2 draw ...

It would seem that he'd not moved too far from his humbler beginnings before the war. He would now set about with a vengeance to change all that.

Endnotes
1. Mems
2. Ditto
3. *Daily Herald,* Tuesday, 21 August 1923
4. *Biggleswade Chronicle,* 4 May 1923
5. *Derby Daily Telegraph,* 14 October 1922
6. *Athletic News,* 6 November 1922
7. *Football Special,* 18 November 1922
8. *Dundee Courier,* 13 January 1923
9. *Sunday Post,* 21 January 1923
10. *Dundee Courier,* 24 January 1923
11. Mems
12. R.W.N., *Montrose Advertiser,* 7 April 1950

Chapter Thirteen

Barson Takes A Battering

'A great powerful fellow who hardly knows his own strength, he is greatly vigorous and apt to be over-impetuous at times yet I have seen him frequently fouled and keep a cool head; and last winter he was the victim of a very unfortunate accident which laid him aside for weeks.' **Profile of Barson, 30 August 1924, *Manchester Football Chronicle.***

'Since I went to United, I've received plenty of hard knocks but never so many as this season. My shins are a mass of bruises at the moment.' **Barson to newspaper correspondent, Christmas 1924.**

(15 September versus Bury 'a small fox terrier ran onto the field causing much amusement and a stoppage of the game before it was eventually captured by Barson.')

BARSON'S STYLE of play, his tendency to throw himself into the action and physically impose himself upon the opposition, was not without consequences for his own health. Opponents were never going to lie down and submit, especially in the lower divisions, but unfortunately for Barson, referees tended to notice him first and act accordingly. Football columnists were generally sympathetic to Barson:

> Huge enthusiastic players are much more likely to come under the notice of referees than men of less physique who are more likely to offend. I have seen Frank Barson fouled twice in the first few minutes of a match without official notice being taken of the incidents.[1]
>
> Frank isn't in good favour with the high authorities simply because his name is forever associated with rough play. Yet it is largely a case of 'give a dog a bad name'. I know Frank very intimately and you can take my word for it that he is never a man to go out of his way deliberately to crock a player. Give Frank a rough and tumble and he'll be delighted, for the simple reason that a trial of real strength is to him a breath of ozone. It is a tonic, just as a fight is to an Irishman, or an argument to a Scot. The trouble comes in when other players go too far with Barson or when other players won't take hard, fair knocks. He then goes too far himself.[2]
>
> In the Second League every game is practically a cup tie and while rough play is absolutely

unnecessary it is essential that players must be prepared to give and receive hard knocks. In this connection may I be allowed to say a word about Barson. The ex-Villa man is, of course, exceedingly well-built and has a broad pair of shoulders, and how often do you hear the cry when he charges at players, 'Send him off!' It is only reasonable to expect that a lightweight bumping against him is likely to get the worst of the bargain and it is not fair to the player that onlookers should be constantly making use of offensive remarks. The most unfortunate part of the business is that many referees nowadays fail to differentiate between the legitimate and the illegitimate shoulder charge.[3]

Which might sound like a case of special pleading; Barson was certainly not without his champions in the national football press, mainly because, unlike opposing fans who now enjoyed barracking him unmercifully, commentators could see his undoubted merits:

'There isn't a centre half anywhere in the land who can break an attack so skilfully; who can pull a high ball to the carpet and keep it there; can nod a ball down to a colleague's toe with his head; who can shoot with such amazing force and accuracy; or who can do such foolish little tricks in the temper-displaying line as this player.'[4]

Nevertheless, tough man or no, the 1923/24 season would see Barson suffer severe injuries that threatened his career.

The campaign began brightly enough with three victories, but from then on times were bleak for United:

four games without a goal scored, before a scrambling 1-1 draw at South Shields, during which Merrick, the Shields goalkeeper, received a blow in the mouth which removed his upper teeth and his top lip had to be stitched. It also saw Barson break down.

'After the match at Ashton Gate against Bristol City on the opening day, Barson complained of pains in the back. He, however, very pluckily continued to struggle on game after game, but last weekend he went under the x-rays and the doctor said, "Stop football at once". His case will require very special treatment and his services will be lost to the club for some time.'[5]

Barson in action

It was indeed severe: 'At Bristol I was up against Fairclough …We had a number of lively duels all fair and square, and after one effort to get the ball we came down together. I fell badly and the pain I suffered was about the most excruciating that I have experienced in football. At first I thought I had sustained a severe strain but later it was discovered that the lower portion of my spine had been partially fractured. I was unable to sit down and as a matter of fact I stood in the corridor of the train all the way home …'[6]

He would be out of action from late September until the end of December, missing 13 games. 'During those dreary weeks of enforced rest I began to think my playing days were over …'

He would return, however, and throw himself into the fray in typical Barsonian fashion, crashing into Fulham's Papworth in mid-January during a 2-1 defeat at Craven Cottage and earning himself a caution and sustained hooting from the London crowd for his pains.

United's results continued to be poor, however; in fact, they would only win three more games all season and end in 14th place, seven points above relegation. By that point, Barson had disappeared again, this time suffering torn ligaments behind his right knee. During a 3-0 loss to Derby County he had to be stretchered off the field, much to the delight of the Derby crowd.

'… Of all men playing today he is least liked by crowds in the Second Division by reason of his vigorous tactics and dangerous play. He is contemptuous of crowds and opinions; he goes onto the field to help his team to win brushing aside the man less endowed with physique and asking no quarter from the biggest opponent. But surely the crowd at Derby on Saturday when they cheered to see him knocked out did not know his injury was so painful or serious as it turned out to be on examination in hospital ...

'The question whether Whitehouse purposely fouled his opponent has been canvassed – the referee gave a free kick, thereby indicating a foul had been committed. Put the matter at its worst though and accept the popular phrase in most cases, "If the forward had not got the half-back, the half-back would have got him ..." It is all Lombard Street to a China orange that Whitehouse had no idea he would do Barson any serious personal injury. In other words – with the worst interpretation on the action of Whitehouse – he did nothing more than attempt to save his own skin ...

'It was characteristic of him that he refused to stay in hospital, insisting on not only being carried to the hotel but on being borne into the room where he could join his Manchester United comrades at tea.'[7]

Barson recalled: 'I was in a bad way. I think I rather alarmed everybody because I would not remain in hospital. Insisted that I rejoin my colleagues at tea. I was in agony at the time. My knee was as big as the proverbial balloon. No one helped to cheer me more than poor Charlie Radford ...'[8]

The emergence of 24-year-old full-back Charlie Radford had been one of the brighter sides to United's disastrous season. A native of Walsall, where he lived with his mother and sister, he was a favourite of Barson's, a tough little player who wasn't afraid to 'take one for the team'. He had finished the 1922/23 season under a six-week suspension, having 'taken the legs away' from a Nelson forward who was about to score.

'Radford was a splendid fellow – just the sort of chap who could help to make you forget your troubles,' Barson recalled.

Radford was one of an increasing number of professional players who, with their relative wealth, were buying motorcars and motorcycles. Travelling in the

Barson training hard

direction of his home in Walsall on 14 July 1924, he accelerated to pass a car, swerved to avoid a cyclist and collided with an electric tramways feeder box. His female passenger was thrown clear but Radford sustained injuries to his face and chest. It wasn't the first time he'd come off his bike, but this time it proved fatal. Under anaesthetic in hospital, his heart (said to be enlarged by more than half a pound, apparently) failed.

Barson later recalled the odd coincidence of Radford's untimely death and that of another of his proteges, Tom Ball, who'd succeeded him at Aston Villa.

'When he [Radford] met his fate Manchester United lost a coming international player – just as Villa did when the shooting tragedy overtook Ball, my successor at Birmingham [Aston Villa].'[9] Ball had been shot by an irate neighbour the previous year in an argument over a dog.

As Barson recovered during the close season of 1924, rumours swirled that he was now preparing to leave United for First Division West Bromwich Albion, rumours strenuously denied by all. Perhaps the idea galvanised the United players. Though they lost the second game of the new 1924/25 season, they then embarked on an unbeaten run lasting until the end of December, racking up 11 wins, four draws and establishing them as favourites to go up. What had changed? Importantly, they were now a settled side, drawing upon a core of 13 players all season.

Alf Steward was now in goal (Mew having left the previous year); Silcock returned from injury to partner Moore for most of the season at full-back; the experienced Mann moved from inside-forward to half-back where, alongside the dependable, hard-working Grimwood, he was a regular partner to Barson.

Up front the team now had a speedy left-winger in McPherson, who became an instant Old Trafford favourite; at centre-forward there was the tall, powerful Henderson (who ended up as top scorer with 14 but who would be surprisingly transferred in January to be replaced by Albert Pape), these complemented by Joe Spence, a dashing, crashing regular down on the right wing.

The action was fast and furious, with Barson generally leading the charge. Against Stoke in September he knocks a forward out with a 'perfectly fair charge' and the crowd yells for a free kick; he then collides with another Stoke player and comes away limping, the crowd baying for a penalty-kick 'but the referee believed the collision to be accidental'; in October there is pandemonium in the crowd at Clapton as United tear into the opposition with Barson again seen to be limping. 'In charging down a hard drive Barson was hurt and he was applauded as he pluckily resumed ...'[10]

At the end of November, United met promotion rivals Derby County in a particularly rough game. Ivan Sharpe reported for *Athletic News*:

> Over 50,000 people gathered at Old Trafford, the home of Manchester United, prepared for pitched battle. They saw for an hour a contest pulsating with thrills, waged with sufficient earnestness to cause friction. They saw the sparks begin to fly as Derby held on grimly to a hard-earned lead, and checked and countered by the quick swoop of their half-backs and an exhibition of swift and relentless tackling by the frantic efforts of Manchester United to resist and defeat this spirited invasion. They saw a good deal of hard, honest effort, and an increasing amount of play that was shady, and ultimately they must have left the ground feeling that great occasion had been ruined by the display of over-keenness and temper, the degrading spectacle of a player being ordered out of the arena.

In this case, the man ordered off was the Derby County centre-forward for a bad foul. With his dismissal, Derby had fallen back and defended, and might have held out for a draw but for a controversial goal.

IN AT THE DEATH

Olney pushed the ball in the air following further free kicks on the home left wing. Undoubtedly he should have fisted the ball away over the bar. A crowd of players descended upon and around him as it fell, and Hanson and Barson were in at the death. Hanson seems to have got the brush but Barson's charge paved the way for the kill. Derby protested; Olney exhibited his ribs to the referee and all and sundry. But what can one see from the centre of the pavilion? We will say it was suspicious and leave the rest with the referee. Even so. Olney should have played for safety.[11]

Other observers saw it differently: 'Sufficient to say now that Olney was badly and painfully fouled before Hanson (most people thought Barson) secured the ball and turned it into the net. In fact, had not the goalkeeper collapsed through his injury he could easily have cleared, for he had the ball between his hands.

'Olney had taken a high lunge at the ball with his fist when he was kneed by Barson. The whistle went and Olney dropped the ball. Other players ceased playing. Hanson, however, kicked the ball through the posts and the referee again blew, this time for a goal, a most unsatisfactory decision.'[12]

Derby County were sufficiently annoyed about Fairclough's dismissal to launch an appeal to the FA that was dismissed, the club being ordered to pay the expenses. Ominously for Barson, however, there had also been a charge brought against him for using 'improper language on the field of play', though it's not clear by whom as the referee hadn't booked him.

In the event, the commission, headed by Barson's old foe Charles Clegg, found that evidence in support of the charge, 'was considered so unsatisfactory that the Commission did not feel justified in dealing with the player'. At the same time they announced ominously that 'had the evidence been proved to their satisfaction they would have had no hesitation in inflicting a serious suspension'.[13]

Early in the new year a bizarre story emerged following Manchester United's 1-0 victory over Chelsea, concerning an alleged threat to Barson from members of his own profession. 'Outside Right' in the *Derby Daily Telegraph* wrote of:

A VEILED ATTACK

Have you read of the veiled attack which is being made on a certain league player, let me quote. 'A certain footballer has for long been under almost constant suspicion. There cannot remain any doubt that he should be. Opponents who have played against him have got so tired of his never ceasing wrong-doing that there is a movement afoot to send a petition to the authorities in order to prevent the player from crocking others. Who is it?

The paper might well have given the name as cast this veiled innuendo about. The player is Frank Barson, and this idea of a round robin – it would never be an open and straightforward petition – originates in the Chelsea camp! You see, I am not afraid of giving facts. The matter may be left to the FA. They know their business, and I cannot credit that they will take any notice of such a dirty piece of work as this is.

Referees have the power to deal with Barson. Let us wait until he gives a referee cause to take drastic action. The very fact that Barson is still playing shows that referees have not yet found him out.[14]

The 'veiled threat', if there indeed had been one, came to nothing. On the field, however, Barson continued to be an object of ire for opposition supporters.

'Barson is a great centre-half … but of all men playing today he is least liked by crowds by reason of his vigorous tactics and dangerous play. [However] he is contemptuous of crowds and opinions; goes on the field to help his team to win, brushing aside the man less endowed with physique, and asking no quarter from the biggest opponent.'[15]

Injuries continued to dog him and the team's progress. He was again absent in early January as United lost to successive games 0-1. The management then decided something drastic was necessary. Centre-forward Henderson, who'd actually scored 14 goals thus far and would remain the club's top scorer that season, was suddenly 'sold'. United offered him to Preston North End and by the end of January he'd gone. A week later they made a dramatic approach to Clapton Orient for the latter's centre-forward, Pape. Neither transfer was without controversy.

Henderson's looked straightforward until it transpired that Preston had paid nothing for him – they had only agreed to take him for £1,760 at the end of the season if he succeeded. In the event, he didn't and so Clapton Orient took him.

The *Lancashire Daily Post* complained,

> Nobody has any grievance. But it is, nevertheless, a somewhat new thing in these days to find it possible for one club to make negotiations for the transfer of a man who is no longer in its employ but is on the transfer list of another. What it amounts to in plain fact is that Henderson was only nominally, not actually, North End's player after the close of the season, which goes to constitute rather the illuminating possibility in the application of the transfer rules.[16]

He'd been loaned in all but name, something the League was trying to prevent. Even odder was the tale of his successor. Having off-loaded Henderson before securing a replacement, manager John Chapman was now anxious to sign someone new, but his search was proving fruitless.

Then someone (could it have been Barson?) mentioned Pape, the Clapton Orient centre-forward who just happened to be playing United in a day's time.

It might not have been a coincidence but Pape was well-known to Frank Barson, who'd trained for some years at Rotherham when Pape had been a forward there. Pape was a big, burly centre-forward who was far from graceful but nevertheless effective on his day. 'In the scientific sense he may not be a footballer,' the *Manchester Guardian* once wrote, 'but he gets goals.'

Contact was made by telephone with Orient's directors, who were amenable to a deal and a fee of £1,070 was swiftly agreed. The Orient players were by then booked onto the morning train to Manchester, and Chapman was told to be at Piccadilly Station to meet them.

The train arrived a little after noon. Pape, who had family in Bolton, readily agreed to the move and he, Chapman and the paperwork decamped to Manchester's General Post Office, where the details were wired through to the Football Association and the Football League at 1.30pm. The deal was confirmed with barely an hour to spare.

'When the teams turned out, just before three o'clock, Pape found himself playing against the men he had travelled from London with,' wrote the *Chronicle*, 'a circumstance he would not have dreamed of, or his old colleagues, an hour or two earlier.'[17]

'When the Orient players were inspecting the ground before the kick-off they asked officials of the Orient club if it was true Pape was to play against them. So fine was the exchange cut. At four o'clock Friday afternoon the Manchester United directors decided to negotiate by telephone with the London club. Terms were arranged, but the player was not seen until just before one o'clock in

Manchester on Saturday. He signed the necessary forms at one o'clock; and telegrams did the rest ...'

Pape, inevitably, scored against his old club in a 4-2 win, 'a capital goal, and contributing to the fall of his suddenly-deserted clubmates. The quicker football finds a remedy for such transactions the better,' opined the *Athletic News*.[18]

The *Manchester Football News* admitted that perhaps such quick transfers on the eve of a match were not in the best interests of the sport, but concluded that 'in this instance it was a case of a serious disease needing a drastic remedy'.

Elsewhere, though, less charitable conclusions were drawn. The *Derby Daily Telegraph* complained that it proved the existing system, 'gives too much power to the clubs with the money bags. The lightning transfer has raised a storm of protest from the football writers and countless thousands of enthusiasts,' they wrote. 'Never before has such an outcry been raised against the transfer system. Even huge fees pall before this exploitation of a system which was unpopular before and is still more hated now.'[19]

Pape's arrival didn't halt the slide in results. It was the absence of Barson that made the crucial difference. The Club Chatter column in the *Derby Daily Telegraph* explained:

> In Praise of Barson. Since Frank Barson fell out of the Manchester United team through groin injury, the club has dropped no less than nine priceless promotion points, and instead of being a match

> hand and one point to the good – as they were then
> – they are now a long way arrears of Derby County.
> If any further proof of Barson's genius pivot were
> required, it can be found here.[20]

It was suggested once again that he was unhappy at the club and wanted to leave. Barson decided to give an interview to set the record straight. He was, he said, 'astonished' at the rumours.

'During the Xmas engagements, which were strenuous, I developed a groin strain, largely owing to the heavy nature of the grounds. I played on, hoping that it would disappear, but it did not … Against Chelsea and Stoke it troubled me very much.'

The club were keen for him to play in an upcoming cup tie and they tried to get him fit. 'Towards the end of the week the strain became worse.' He didn't play in the cup tie at Sheffield but came back against Oldham, though had to leave the field 20 minutes before the finish owing to the strain reasserting itself.

'Did I play again too soon? I am afraid I did … I have been ordered to rest from the field …'[21]

He remained confident his team would gain promotion, however, and stressed he would be ready for the run-in. He was reinstated in April against Derby and though they lost that day (Barson was reported to have said to his team-mates in the dressing room afterwards, 'Never mind boys. It looks bad at the moment but this race isn't over yet') they would not lose again that season and ultimately gained the much-sought-after promotion as runners-up to Second Division champions Leicester City.

The position was clinched via a 4-0 win over Port Vale at Old Trafford which left them two points clear of Derby (who'd suffered a calamitous collapse) with a superior goal-difference and only one game to play. The *Athletic News* columnist noted:

> A scene of enthusiasm, remarkable for a Second Division ground, was witnessed at Old Trafford after the game with Port Vale. The official return of the attendance was forty thousand and one, and the odd gentleman must have been delighted he was there. It was all a picture in league history to be long remembered and often to be recalled when the embers burn low and the last pipe is smoked.[22]

Derby Daily Telegraph's Club Chatter columnist was also on hand to note:

BARSON'S TRIBUTE

Frank Barson had tribute paid to his popularity at Old Trafford last week, when his clubmates surrounded him at the close of their game with Port Vale and congratulated him on leading them to promotion. Frank declares that he has never served a club that could take defeat with a smile as do the directors of Manchester United. It is something which players do appreciate.[23]

United's emergency signing, Albert Pape, would later sum Barson up:

The most inspiring captain and most useful field general soccer has known since the war. They had to tape him up with a mile of bandages, owing to serious groin trouble. He was not fit to play in a mid-week friendly, let alone for the most strenuous struggle from promotion of the season, but he played like a hero and supported us all by word and deed. I will always take my hat off to Frank! [24]

Endnotes

1. *Manchester Football Chronicle*, 30 August 1924
2. *Derby Daily Telegraph*, 1 November 1924
3. *Manchester Football News*, September 1923
4. Ditto
5. *Manchester Football News*, 13 October 1923
6. Mems
7. *Derby Daily Telegraph*, 18 February 1924
8. Mems
9. Ditto
10. *Manchester Football Chronicle*, September 1924
11. *Athletic News*, 1 December 1924
12. *Derby Daily Telegraph*, 1 December 1924
13. *Sheffield Daily Telegraph*, 3 January 1925
14. *Derby Daily Telegraph*, 10 January 1925
15. *Derby Daily Telegraph*, Monday, 18 February 1924
16. *Lancashire Daily Post*, 29 August 1925
17. *Manchester Football Chronicle*, 9 February 1925
18. *Athletic News*, 9 February 1925
19. *Derby Daily Telegraph*, February 1925
20. *Derby Daily Telegraph*, 14 March 1925
21. *Thomsons Weekly News*, 14 March 1925
22. *Athletic News*, 27 April 1925
23. *Derby Daily Telegraph*, 2 May 1925
24. *The People*, 3 January 1926

Chapter Fourteen

Back in the Big Time

*'By the way, many people regard Barson as a
kind of football bandit, a man whose hand is
against everyone and everyone's hand against
him. Never was there a greater mistake. He
is one of the jolliest, nicest, most affable, good-
hearted and genial men in football.*

*'He is a bit dour on the field? Well, yes: but
as a companion he is splendid, and is very
popular among his fellow players. Perhaps
silly people who talk as though he were a
species of hooligan will kindly noted those
remarks. They are made by one who enjoyed
Barson's friendship.'* **Jesse Pennington,
Topical Times, 1922.**

*'Quite a number of the boys tell me that
gardening is one of the finest exercises for*

the close season. Frankly I prefer tennis. Gardening is a super pastime – just rather too strenuous for poor delicate fellows like us. I am glad to say that I am now settled in my new home and though the front room wants a bit of attention Mrs B and I are congratulating ourselves upon our labours. We had a house-warming the other day and you can bet there was a strong football atmosphere at the gathering.' **Barson writing to *Thomson's Weekly News*, 2 July 1927.**

THE MANCHESTER United players will have celebrated their promotion in various ways, though perhaps not quite as wildly as Barson's half-back partner Jack Grimwood. ('A professional footballer, John Barton Grimwood, of Manchester United, was fined at South Shields yesterday for drunkenness and improper conduct.'[1])

There is the legendary story of Barson celebrating securing United's First Division status by taking up the licence of a public house in Manchester, gifted to him by one of United's directors, Davies, a prosperous brewer, as a reward. The tale goes that the pub/hotel was in Ardwick Green South, called the George and Dragon, and that Barson had already started packing up his Grimesthorpe home when he paid an exploratory visit. Manchester United supporters had heard the news and flocked along to celebrate with him but after a quarter of an hour's mayhem, with scores of eager folk drinking his health, Barson decided it wasn't for him. He apparently turned to the 'head-waiter' and said, 'Do you want this place?' before handing over the keys and retreating to Sheffield.

The origin of the tale would appear to be lifelong Manchester United supporter and *Manchester Evening Chronicle* reporter Alf Clarke. Clarke was also the official Manchester United reporter for the *Chronicle*, and a great fan of Barson's. His inside knowledge of the club and its affairs was unrivalled and after he perished at Munich in the 1958 disaster, his ashes were scattered over the Old Trafford pitch.

Clarke claimed to have seen every one of Barson's matches and rated him, 'the finest centre-half-back I have ever seen'. His account of Barson's refusal to become a publican has to be taken as accurate, therefore, although it's possible that Barson already had a 'licensed business' in Sheffield. (It had been one of the sticking points in his refusal to go to live in Birmingham.)

Clarke told the pub story to illustrate what he considered to be Barson's dislike of flattery and undue fuss. It also demonstrates a tendency to light-heartedness on Barson's part. In fact, Barson was considered by his team-mates as something of a wit, the dressing-room joker. Manchester United trainer Pullar, in a March 1927 edition of *Topical Times*, commented:

> When he was with us Billy Meredith was the chief
> mischief-maker but when he left Old Trafford the

job became Frank Barson's. I have despaired of
Frank mending his ways ...

Most of the stories Pullar told could well have been lifted
from *Tom Brown's Schooldays*, consisting late night pillow
fights or the rather strange occurrence such as when he
found Barson and Charlie Radford in their bedroom
one night arguing over whose nose cast a bigger shadow
against the wall (apparently electric light hadn't reached
Chingford where they were staying and candles were the
only source of illumination).

As anyone who has played for a sports team on a regular
basis will know, 'banter' and 'humour' are generally of the
juvenile kind, and the jokes rarely travel. 'Practical' jokes
are also standard fare and intended to bind individuals
into the team set-up, hence the unpopularity of team
members who try to remain aloof and apart, Neil McBain
being a prime example.

Nevertheless, anodyne though the tales might be,
they run counter to that aspect of the Barson legend that
saw him depicted as a razor-wielding gang leader. That
particular image was a combination of two tales, the
first told by Billy Walker when recalling Barson in his
autobiography *Soccer in the Blood*, and the second by Dixie
Dean when talking to Radio Merseyside in the 1970s.

Walker wrote,

> Frank had no inhibitions on the field or off it and
> an indication of that is that he was never ashamed
> of numbering among his friends the notorious
> Fowler brothers who were hanged for murder.

THE NEW LODGER.

Thereby, if you will forgive the pun, hangs a tale. One Saturday we were playing at Tottenham and there, as we entered our dressing room, was a letter addressed to Frank Barson, Aston Villa FC. After reading it through, he turned to us and said: 'Listen, lads, these are the sorts of pals you want.'

The letter read:

> 'Dear Frank, best wishes for today. Hope you win
> the cup this year although we won't be there to see
> it, good luck.'
>   It was from the Fowler Brothers, literally from
> the condemned cell.[2]

Dixie Dean's account of his first on-field encounter
with Barson, given in some 1970s interviews for Radio
Merseyside, developed the Fowler theme and embellished
it. He claimed that fellow professionals feared Barson for
his off-field as well as on-field activities.

'Sammy Chedgzoy warned me about one of the
United players and said, "Whatever happens today don't
put a boot near this man ... Don't upset him"... He was
talking about a feller called Frank Barson. Now this
Barson was also head of the razor gang from Sheffield.
They were going round the country in the racing lark
demanding money with a razor.'[3]

Dean's claim that Barson was the leader of a 'razor
gang' was as unreliable as his footballing memory.
According to Dean, during the match in question, Barson
felled him with a punch shortly after play commenced but
that retaliation was inflicted by Everton's inside-right,
Bobby Irvine, whom Dean describes as 'a good, hard
kid who would have a go at anybody'. Irvine, according
to Dean, then kicked Barson so hard in the ribs and on
the jaw that Barson was stretchered off.

In fact, Dean and Barson only met twice on-field,
in 1926 and 1927. On the second occasion Irvine wasn't

playing and in 1926, during an ill-tempered 0-0 draw, it was Barson who shook up Irvine, presumably in retaliation for the punch Irvine had certainly thrown back in Barson's Aston Villa days. Barson was not carried off on either occasion.

A more accurate description of the events in the particular match was as follows in the *Liverpool Echo*:

> One of the best things of the match was a good solid shoulder charge from Batten on to Barson and it was followed a second later by a similar clumping charge by Dean on the same man, who rolled over three times. Barson took his gruel without demur, which was exactly how Everton took Barson's earlier offence. When Spence fell in the penalty area pretty badly hurt, Barson tried to work off the Sunderland cup-tie tricks. He raced up to the referee and begged him to consult the linesman, but this referee, Mr Mee of Mansfield, would have none of it ...[4]

Where Walker's story is concerned, false memory seems to be at work once again: Aston Villa played Spurs in the FA Cup in 1921, while the Fowler brothers were hanged some four years later following a widely publicised trial.

The Fowlers were part of – perhaps the most prominent members of – the gang culture that dominated post-First World War cities, Sheffield in particular, and they might well have written to Barson as letter-writing from the condemned cell was a common feature of the time and usually given prominence in popular newspapers, although had they actually written to Barson it would have been headline news. That Frank Barson, a very prominent professional footballer in his 30s, would have been involved with such a motley crew is stretching credulity, however.

Interestingly, at about the same time the Fowlers were being hanged for murder, Barson's younger brother Sydney was being sentenced to three months in gaol for assaulting a policeman along with three other Grimesthorpe young men in a pub brawl. Barson's background was not pretty, but it certainly wasn't homicidal.

What Barson actually got up to once the football season ended was disappointingly mundane. He rarely revealed much about his off-field activities, but whenever he did they tended to consist of walking, fishing or playing bowls.

He once outlined his summer regime for the readers of *All Sports*:

> I like Lincolnshire, and here is my programme.
> Up very early to gather mushrooms for breakfast,
> then to the river and spend a day on the bank. Back
> to the village, a sound meal, and then a game of
> dominoes with the locals in the local meeting place,
> the usual 'night-cap' and afterwards to bed.

'The occasional game of tennis was included as his pre-season warm up but golf and cricket he positively disliked.'[5]

Barson was the focal point of a good-natured crowd of United players, some of whom would adjourn to his house

FOOTBALL CHRONICLE. SATURDAY, DECEMBER 13, 1924.

UNITED'S FIRST DIVISION DREAM.

FIRST DIVISION

MANCHESTER UNITED

PLEASE DONT WAKE ME

(in Manchester, where he ultimately agreed to settle in 1927) following arduous away trips, often at midnight. There they would indulge in one of his favourite steaming hot-pot suppers prepared by his wife, and be abused by his foul-mouthed parrot.

In the wider football world, however, significant changes were occurring, not least of which was the new offside rule, introduced at the start of the 1925/26 season. It would impact significantly on Barson himself.

The old rule stipulated that for a forward to be onside when receiving a forward pass, three opposing players (usually the goalkeeper and two defenders) had to be between him and his opponents' goal. This meant forwards had to take their position from the more advanced full-back; the other back was thus able to act effectively as a sweeper behind him and it was thus much easier for defenders to 'spring the offside trap'. Consequently, the game became increasingly broken up and attacks and goals diminished. It had also allowed the centre-half much more freedom to create and build attacks.

In June 1925 the Council of the English Football Association, having considered limiting the offside area to within 40 yards of each goal line or alternatively reducing the opponents from three to two, decided on the latter plan.

Now any misjudgement on behalf of the defending team meant leaving a forward through one-on-one with the keeper. An immediate effect saw forwards afforded more room in which to move, as the game became stretched. In time, short passing gave way to longer balls 'over the top' of the defence and subsequently saw the emergence of the 'stopper' centre-half, who thus became a defender first and foremost.

In October 1925 Barson penned an article for a local paper entitled 'Attack Is The Best Defence', in which he touched on the new rule and its possible deleterious effects on the game.

'The charm of the game,' he wrote, 'is in the whole-hearted attack: that is, offensive methods in which the half-backs as well as the forwards play their part.'[6] He was worried that, as a consequence of the new rule, with attack being given more prominence, defences would respond in kind and the game become even more restricted. He was right.

Already since the war, he claimed, clubs had tended to concentrate more and more on defensive tactics which had resulted in a dearth of 'attacking centre-halves', such as Manchester United's Charlie Roberts – the type of player that he, Barson, had watched as a youth and so successfully copied.

He added to his analysis a couple of weeks later in a *Liverpool Echo* piece beneath the headline, 'Centre-Forward Trouble'.[7] Managers, he said, had quickly got used to seeking out men who could simply score goals while contributing little else. It was easy, however, to mark simple goalscoring individuals but what was needed were all-round leaders of the line, men who could distribute the ball, give and take passes, etc. This was partly because the centre-half, the key position, was now finding himself more on the 'defensive'. Barson was beginning to sense the shifting tactical sands.

In the same month, *Athletic News* conducted a survey of players to see how centre-backs were coping with the new law. 'The player with the biggest problem is the centre-back. The backs, as far as English experiences go to date, have been unable in most cases to cope with the new order without the help of the centre-half-back … Can he check the crop of goals that have been recorded to centre-forwards? He is in for hard work …'

Barson was sanguine in his response: 'I would have preferred the 40 yards offside scheme, but I am convinced that the best method is to play the old game with the half-

backs well up the field and supporting attack. The centre-forward must be ready to come more into combination with the centre-half.' At the same time he acknowledged that the centre-half is 'certainly more heavily burdened'.[8]

Barson's Manchester United team would suffer from the very deficiencies he was warning against, however, mainly because they lacked the skilful attacking players necessary (possessing neither prolific scorers nor versatile playmakers) to keep opposing sides on the back foot. The coming campaign would see just two United players break into double scoring figures: the newly acquired Rennox would notch 17 goals, and the speedy McPherson would manage 16. The team as a whole would score just 66 goals. Champions Huddersfield, meanwhile, hit 92 goals, third-placed Sunderland 96 and Sheffield United would top 100 goals. Even Manchester City, who would be relegated, scored 89 goals. What United did have, however, was a solid defence, and it would be the basis for much of their early success.

West Ham full-back W. Henderson commented: 'There have been many matches this season where a team has scored three or four goals yet lost the points. The explanation may be that these teams have been concentrating too severely on defence. I believe that attack is still the best defence and that it is the half-back's main job to keep in touch with his forwards. That this is still possible, Barson and one or two others have demonstrated. Barson is still an attacking centre-half, but he generally contrives to be on the premises when danger threatens. That is the whole art of centre-half play, of course.'[9]

In terms of personnel, Clarence Hilditch would return to partner Barson in the half-back line, along with Mann, who would edge out Grimwood. Full-backs Silcock and Moore continued to be as solid as ever, while up-front Pape disappeared as swiftly as he arrived, sold to Fulham, Rennox replaced Lochhead (who was also sold) and McPherson, naturally a winger, operated largely as a dashing centre-forward.

The team struggled at first, using some 16 players in the first nine games, losing four and drawing three. After a fractious defeat at Leeds, however, they went on an unbeaten run of eight games, winning six and ascending almost to the top of the division. By November they were third in the table, boasting the best defence in the league, having let in just 20 goals in 17 games.

Their methods were simple – swift, direct, attacking play, the ball shifted forward as soon as possible to exploit McPherson's pace, a solid defence built squarely around Barson. They had, in fact, adapted to the new rule change far more quickly than many others. Ivan Sharpe had noticed:

> Manchester United have few frills, but it is a mistake to write them down merely as a workmanlike side, a combination of rush and tumble concerned only in crashing the ball through the goal. Judging by the displays I have seen the Old Trafford team give to date, they owe their advance to half-back play, and this half-back work is on a higher plane than the majority of clubs I have seen this season. Barson, in the mood, is without peer in combining constructive and defensive play. Mann has always been as crafty in attack as dour in defence; Hilditch is consistent, if not brilliant. Here is Manchester United's source of strength, and there is subtlety as well as spirit.[10]

With United ascending to the upper reaches of the First Division, and with Barson the stand-out celebrity in their line-up, he was clearly revelling in the spotlight:

The ground was ice-bound. The players could not turn, could not keep their feet, were reluctant to risk a fall. Consequently, the intermediate play of the winners calls for high praise. The master, of course, was Barson. He dominated the middle of the field in the true centre-half-back way. Opponents seemed to stand in awe. He often had too much room to work in. Why, on one occasion he juggled with the ball on his head in a Cinquevalli way, bobbing it up six times – a friend said seven! – before he touched it, finally, over the head of Roscamp, the nearest adversary, and proceeded to prance past him and slip the ball along the touchline with delightful accuracy – a little side show in itself. But there were extra turns. Barson headed back and passed back to the goalkeeper in a manner that suggested the friendly exhibition game and roused the 33,000 shivering spectators to smiles and cheers because of his nonchalance. Blackburn seemed merely to be looking on. 'There when wanted,' as the comedians used to sing.[11]

He also wasted no time in reasserting his methods on old acquaintances. Two of United's first four fixtures were against his old club Aston Villa, where Billy Walker was now an established, much-loved star striker. Villa had started the season with a mighty bang, beating Burnley (albeit reduced to ten-men) 10-0. Barson clearly was in no mind to see that happen to him and his United team.

Walker remembered the game well: 'Before the match he came to me and warned me, "Now Billy don't hang onto that ball today or you'll be for it." I retorted, "I'll hold it as long as I want Frank," and we went out on the field.

'After about ten minutes we got away and scored the first goal. Frank as usual looked round and rolled up his sleeves, which was the sign to everyone who knew him that he meant business.

'"If you want a battle, the battle's on," he said with a grin. I was keeping a weather eye on him but about ten minutes after the second half had begun I had had a quick look round to see that he was not in the vicinity, I got the ball and went past Ray Bennion. I pushed the ball out to Arthur Dorrell, saw him centre to the far post and – whoosh, something hit me like a ton of bricks and I finished on the track.

'Of course it was Frank. He had kept his promise, yet he came into our dressing room after the match to enquire: "How are you lad? I'm sorry. You know I wouldn't hurt a hair on your head!"

'It took me three weeks to get over that little reminder. What a player he was – one of the greatest centre-halves ever – but oh what a terrier on the field!'[12]

In the same match, George Stephenson, Clem's younger brother, was also 'in the wars', having been led off for a spell with blood streaming down his face. 'After the match Stephenson was interviewed and said he did not remember anything for half an hour. When he got to the dressing room the wound, over the left eye, had to be stitched by the doctor, he having lost a lot of blood and was suffering terrific pains in his head.'[13]

It wouldn't be the last time that Barson targeted his young Villa protégé – the following year Barson meted

the same treatment to Walker. To quote Harricus in the
Athletic News:

> [Barson] is the perfect artist with the ball, clever
> with head and foot, but he participated in an
> unfortunate incident after 20 minutes play that
> resulted in the play of Walker being affected for
> the rest of the game.[14]
>
> After a few minutes he [Walker] resumed amid
> cheers but the crowd for some time continued to
> boo Barson every time he touched the ball. Such a
> demonstration against a player on his own ground
> has rarely been seen.[15]

Understandably, the attention paid to him and his on-
field activities would become more intense. His Liverpool
critic in particular noted in a 2-0 defeat of Leeds United:

> THE TACTICS OF BARSON RESENTED
> Except for the first 15 minutes, there was little
> convincing football in the game between Leeds
> United and Manchester United, owing to play
> being too keen and too many free kicks. After
> Jennings had scored for Leeds he came into contact
> with Baston, who was continually hissed and booed
> for adopting tactics which met with the disapproval
> of 25,000 people.[16]

Barson would comment on the game in *Thomson's
Weekly News*:

BARRACKING OF BARSON

He did bump into Jennings with vigour early on in the game … There were other bumps and trips which were worse and Barson was not the culprit. But Barson got the barracking … Barson continued undismayed. At half-time he was jeered and at the conclusion of the game he got another dose but other offenders – on both sides – were forgotten.

'A nice crowd; oh yes, a nice crowd,' said Barson to me afterwards. "But I am not worried. Do you know a good round of jeering is as good as a good round of cheering?" Yes, this is the worst I have had this season …[17]

Manchester United were never going to win the First Division title, however. Barson was injured again in mid-season, missing nine of 11 between mid-December and the start of March, including a 6-1 defeat by Manchester City – at Old Trafford!

By mid-March, they were still in touch with the leaders, nine points off the top with three games in hand, but they came to a juddering halt against Huddersfield Town, the eventual champions, losing 5-0. After that, they would lose seven more times, including a 7-0 walloping by Blackburn Rovers (during which prolific centre-forward Ted Harper scored four times) and their league challenge collapsed. They would finish in ninth position.

It would be a different story in the FA Cup that season, however; in fact, the United campaign that season would prove to be both the high and the low point in Barson's Manchester United career.

Endnotes

1. *Lancashire Evening Post*, 16 June 1925
2. Billy Walker, *Soccer in the Blood* (London: Stanley Paul, 1960), p.28
3. Richard Holt, *"Heroes of the North ' in Sport and Identity in the North of England*, Jeff Hill and Jack Williams (eds.) (Keele University Press, 1996), pp. 137–164
4. *Liverpool Echo*, 20 March 1926
5. *All Sports*, 16 July 1927
6. *Diss Express and Lincolnshire Echo*, 9 October 1925
7. *Liverpool Echo*, 25 October 1925
8. *Athletic News*, 15 October 1925
9. *Mansfield Reporter*, 29 January 1926
10. *Athletic News*, 30 November 1925
11. *Athletic News*, 30 November 1925
12. Billy Walker, *Soccer in the Blood* (London: Stanley Paul, 1960), p.29
13. *Birmingham Daily Gazette*, 3 September 1925
14. *Athletic News*, 3 October 1926
15. *Sports Argus*, 2 October 1926
16. *Liverpool Echo*, 3 October 1925
17. *Thomson's Weekly News*, 10 October 1925

Chapter Fifteen

The Barson Bump

'There is tiny red imp on my ash tray. He is calling down a megaphone. Some such little devil has settled times on the shoulder of Frank Barson and sung into his ear: "Can you stand for that?"' **Athletic News, Monday, 21 September 1925.**

'He was brought up in the Barnsley school of football thought and one wit has said Manchester United might well be dubbed "Barnsley United" this season ... He captains a side which is fast and extremely energetic. Plain, unvarnished football – robust and strong in shoulder-work – is played.' **Sheffield Daily Telegraph, 26 March 1926.**

MANCHESTER UNITED'S cup campaign of 1926 was something of a protracted struggle.

Against Second Division Port Vale and before a capacity crowd of 20,000, United – without Barson, who was ill with tonsillitis – went 3-0 up but were pegged back to 3-2 and just managed to hold on.

They then met Tottenham Hotspur at White Hart Lane, once again without Barson, and again contrived to throw away a lead. Jacques in the *Athletic News* enthused:

> The cup tie of Saturday must surely rank as one of the most interesting and exciting events witnessed by the Tottenham crowd in recent times. There was no wind to aid the winners of the toss, and the field was in favour of the men until light rain in the second half made the turf a trifle slippery.
>
> There came an opening which astonished and thrilled the assembly – two goals to the visiting side in the first 15 minutes; a valiant effort and rally and two goals to the home side in the next quarter hour, an even and desperate goalless struggle for the rest of the match. Greater efforts no men could have made on the field of football.[1]

The replay at Old Trafford was less spectacular and this time, in a hard, fast match, with the defences generally masters of the situation, United established a 2-0 lead and didn't allow Spurs back into the game. United's 'direct methods' had now seen them earn a quarter-final clash with joint league leaders Sunderland, who along with Huddersfield were considered the best bet to lift the trophy.

Once again United were drawn away, and this time it was they who went two goals down and had to drag themselves back, not once, but twice when they forced an equaliser in the last few minutes to earn a 3-3 draw. Barson played, although he was said to be feeling the effects of his earlier illness. In fact, he had the misfortune to concede Sunderland's second goal. Winger Death had drawn keeper Mew out of his six-yard box and shot across goal, the ball skidding off Barson's foot into the net as he retreated to cover.

The replay at Old Trafford would be controversial and Barson would once again be at the centre of a storm. Sunderland went 2-1 down, but towards the end had an equaliser by their prolific forward Dave Halliday disallowed. Halliday broke away from United's midfield, cut in skilfully and shot sharply. The United goalkeeper parried the ball but was beaten to it as Halliday rushed in to give the ball a parting kick into the net.

'The referee was on the spot and signalled goal, and there were the mutual hand-shakings and demonstrations of joy that usually in these days accompany the scoring of a goal in Association football.'

It was then that Frank Barson decided to give 20th-century football fans a preview of today's VAR system. The *Sunderland Gazette* ran a headline 'An Injustice Has Been Done' and outlined what happened:

> Suddenly Barson, the Manchester United captain, was seen to speak to the referee, who crossed the

field to consult with one linesman, and repeated the process to the other. The result was the signalling of goal kick. To the observer the goal certainly appeared legitimate, and the only grounds of appeal that seemed possible were whether the Manchester goalkeeper had been impeded and hustled into goal before he could get the ball or the scorer had handled. It was later stated that the goal was disallowed for Halliday handling – an informality that apparently had escaped the notice of the referee. Undoubtedly the escape was lucky for Manchester, for their defence had been well beaten.[2]

The incident was recalled almost 30 years later by a Scottish columnist called Gable Ender who was present:

In a replayed English cup tie between Manchester United and Sunderland, I saw the referee hypnotised by Frank Barson, pivot and captain of the United. Barson was playing in grand fashion. His voice ruled almost as much as did the referee's whistle. Davie Halliday, now Dundee United's manager, was Sunderland's centre-forward. He was at his best, giving Barson as much as he wanted to do.

Halliday then 'scored'.

Then came an incident – Barson seized the referee by an arm and walked him around while the vast

Barson own goal versus Sunderland 1926

crowd lapsed into silence. As the pair walked so
did Barson expostulate, gesticulate, and point. The
'ref' could not shake himself free. Barson appealed
for offside against Halliday, contending that when
the outside-right let loose the scoring shot, Davie
was offside. Personally, I thought that Halliday was
well in play and the referee's decision correct. But
the official was so affected by Barson's personality
and persuasive eloquence that he changed his
mind and gave a free kick against Sunderland for
offside. That decision created a wild hullaballoo.
Sunderland protested in vain. United's following
cheered. The decision sealed the fate of Sunderland
in the cup tie. It also sounded the beginning of the
end of the referee in big football. I can see Barson
yet walking the official about and practically
hypnotising him.[3]

To many observers, particularly those on Merseyside, Barson seemed on occasions to get away with behaviour that other players might not. The *Liverpool Echo* columnist Bee was a regular critic, labelling a group of United fans 'the Barson clan' who 'watched their be-all and end-all with extreme care, almost to devotion'.[4]

Bee made reference to an occasion during an Everton match when Barson had tried unsuccessfully to pressure the referee into changing his mind over a couple of offside decisions: 'But [the referee] would not listen to the voice of the charmer. Why should he? Had he not read how Barson persisted till a cup-tie referee changed his mind concerning an incident under his very nose?'[5]

In the Sunderland quarter-final, Bee continued: 'the real Kelly was out of touch with the game for a full hour, and maybe the bump he got from Barson right under the referee's nose did not hearten his game. He asked the referee, "What about it?" and the referee was tongue-tied! He could have blown his whistle. Instead he let the incident go as if nothing had happened. Sunderland were unlucky to go out.'[6]

Nevertheless, United were now through to an FA Cup semi-final where they would meet arch-rivals Manchester City, a team that had managed to almost literally bury their FA Cup opponents beneath an avalanche of goals: four against Corinthians (after a replay), four against Huddersfield (the reigning Football League champions), 11 against Crystal Palace and six against Clapton Orient.

Who would win the game was a difficult call. Coming into the semi-final, United were sitting sixth in the league, while City were almost doomed to relegation.

According to *Athletic News*'s Ivan Sharpe, United had become essentially, 'a cup-fighting team ... fast and spirited. I shall not do them an injustice if I say they have little pretension to class.'

City, on the other hand, possessed ball players and played with greater style and cohesion. That had been apparent earlier in the season when they'd produced one of the shocks of the campaign: a 6-1 thrashing of United at Old Trafford, a result Ivan Sharpe had called 'amazing'. Manchester City would prosper, Sharpe felt, 'if they could escape the full effects of United's shock tactics'.[7]

It was the old football conundrum: would prolific scorers defeat redoubtable defenders? The odds were slightly in United's favour and they did possess the one charismatic character in Frank Barson. Manchester City's Sam Cowan, Tom Johnson and Jimmy McMullan (whom City had signed no more than a month before for £4,700) were fine, skilful players, but the object of attention, for good or ill, would be Barson.

The football writer Perseus in the *Lancashire Evening Post* listened in to City supporters on the train up to Sheffield:

> Doesn't matter whether 'e's in or not, if 'e only knew it. But 'e'll know tonight. I 'ope the best team wins, but I 'ope it's th' City – an' we'll show Barson where he gets off. Uni'ed aren't a bad side – but Barson! – MYSELF![8]

Barson would not disappoint them. Interviewed on the day of the game, he suggested that United had a plan ...

THE BARSON BUMP

'Derby games are always very funny things and you can never tell what is going to happen. When the Derby games are cup ties the issue is even more uncertain. Despite this, I am in no way worried about the game. I am equally certain that Manchester City are as sanguine as we are and I am perfectly satisfied to await the game and let that be the sole judge of our efforts.

'You cannot say that Manchester United have had an easy passage to the semi-final; we have had to fight our way there and we are quite content to carry on the struggle one step further.

'When we enter the arena we shall know exactly what we are about to try to do. You can take it from me that we are not satisfied with 90 minutes of football; the team that wins matches is the team which studies every point beforehand and goes onto the field with a definite plan of campaign. We have had a plan against every opponent that we have met so far. We shall have one for Manchester City. What plan? Ah well, I suppose you will be at the game; if so you must wait and see.'[9]

Whatever it was, the plan clearly didn't work from the very start. The *Sheffield Daily Telegraph* reporter wrote:

> 15 minutes in, City's Hicks put in sharp, low drive and, after stopping the ball, Steward had to throw it out of play for safety. From the ensuing flag kick a goal was scored, Browell getting his head to the ball in a scramble in the goalmouth. This goal led to an unseemly demonstration by the United players, a number of whom wildly gesticulated in front of the referee and followed him many yards,

233

Barson clashes with Billy Walker

while Steward ran almost to the half-way line to give his version.[10]

Ivan Sharpe was certain:

Manchester United made quite a scene about it but I deemed it a good goal. Twas said that someone was pushed but I saw no such persuasion, and when Browell headed the goal from Hicks's corner-kick the referee was within three yards of the incident. The ball sailed to Browell and Browell headed in.

234

It was forced out again but there was no doubt that it had been just over the line.[11]

Manchester United seemed to shiver in their shoes. They never struck a winning gait. They sliced the ball and slipped and stumbled. Their dash and devil ran to waste so that their spirit was steadily sapped. The quite alarming energy that they had generated to the cost of Spurs and Sunderland was never developed and hurled into a collective effort. It was all individual helter-skelter.[12]

The *Derby Daily Telegraph* columnist agreed: 'Manchester United were utterly innocuous; City won in the commonest of canters – won how they liked, and largely because they were keyed up to the occasion, adopted the right policy and stuck to it, and because every man in their attack was a marksman and had confidence.'

He added, 'For the first time I have seen Frank Barson overrun, reduced to ball-chasing, and finally to that much-discussed foul. It was not a savoury incident, but there were others far worse.'[13]

'Much discussed' is no exaggeration, as it would lead to severe consequences for Frank Barson.

The incident came at a crucial moment in the game. Early in the second half, City were leading 1-0 and their half-back line of Pringle (Billy Meredith's son-in-law), McMullen (already in the wars and sporting a badly cut and plastered eye) and Sammy Cowan were controlling the game. Barson appeared to decide that something drastic was necessary. Ivan Sharpe:

Players Barson Bumped

THE BARSON FOUL

So the second vital moment of the match is reached, and is an ugly one, for the imp about which I have written suddenly shouted into the ear of Barson, and Cowan was knocked flat – down and out. A merciless crash it was, and altogether too vigorous. Cowan lay flat; Barson crouched on his knees, and the crowd, suspecting the 'old soldier,' roared the more.[14]

The *Daily Mail* termed it: 'An Ugly Incident:

Early in the second half, with play in midfield, Barson charged Cowan, as the latter leapt for the ball, so violently that the City centre-half was stretched out. For minutes, there was every indication of an ugly scene, so incensed were some of the City players. The crowd, too, demonstrated loudly and for a long time 'booed' Barson whenever he touched the ball. Before play was resumed, the referee apparently admonished the United captain.[15]

The *Sunday Post* writer commented:

There was no necessity for this clash. Cowan fell like a log and Barson was slightly injured. The crowd set up a derisive howl and referee Barrett cautioned Barson, after which the United captain returned to his previous game, which was scientific, clever and effective. But the crowd barracked him intermittently and he got a lively reception when he came off the field.[16]

Not everyone thought that Barson was unaffected by the incident. Sharpe seemed to see it as a turning point: 'It was a vital moment because Barson thereafter was not the same man …'

Until then he had 'generally got the ball and had been quite a power about the premises. Now he, too, was nervy – cautious and subdued. And when that happened the bottom fell out of the United defence.'[17]

Barson even contrived to miss the ball ('fancy that!') that permitted Hicks to send one more gilt-edged offering to Browell, who scored City's second. Four minutes later Roberts ran through on his own and had his shot turned against a post by Steward, whence it bounded across the goal and into the net. The game was over, along with Manchester United's season. The club would not reach another semi-final for 20 years.

Barson remained unrepentant concerning the foul, however. After the match he commented, 'There were much worse offences committed than that,' but went on to congratulate City. 'They had a better side and some good inside-forwards. They have played splendid football and deserve their victory. My hope is that City win the cup.' They didn't, of course, and were duly relegated.

The 'flagrant and foolish' Barson affair was concluded almost a month later, when on 21 April it was announced that the FA had suspended him for two months, commencing from 3 May. He was thus free to play until the end of the season, the suspension actually amounting to a hefty fine.

There was speculation as to the 'peculiar nature' of the punishment as the referee had only booked him, but it seemed a further report had been sent to the FA. It was clear, however, that the threat of severe punishment made a season before had now come back to haunt him.

In the *Yorkshire Evening Post* of 21 April it read:

> The nature of the offence is not stated but Barson, though one of the greatest half-backs in football, has a reputation for impulsiveness and does not always keep a guard upon his tongue so that the reason for the disciplinary action is open to conjecture.[18]

The *Green 'Un* read:

> Barson Case Echo: In arriving at their decision [the Emergency Committee of the FA] have regard to the previous decisions affecting the conduct of the player on the field of play.[19]

Interestingly, the *Athletic News* tried to reassure readers that Barson was not being targeted by the game's rulers. It cautioned:

> It is a mistake to assume, however, that the severity of the sentence arises from the fact that more than one member of the FA Council was present at the

match. This would be quite an unjust attitude to adopt and distinctly uncomplimentary to referees.[20]

No one, however, certainly not Barson, was convinced.

Endnotes

1. *Athletic News*, 1 February 1926
2. *Sunderland Daily Echo and Shipping Gazette*, 25 February 1926
3. *Montrose, Arbroath and Brechin review, and Forfar and Kincardineshire Advertiser*, 17 February 1955
4. *Liverpool Echo*, 22 March 1926
5. *Liverpool Echo*, 22 March 1926
6. *Liverpool Echo*, 25 February 1926
7. *Athletic News*, 22 March 1926
8. *Lancashire Evening Post* Sports Causerie, The railway train philosopher, 3 April 1926
9. *All Sports Illustrated*, 27 March 1926
10. *Sheffield Daily Telegraph*, 29 March 1926
11. *Athletic News*, 29 March 1926
12. *Athletic News*, 29 March 1926
13. *Derby Daily Telegraph*, 3 April 1926
14. *Athletic News*, 29 March 1926
15. *Daily Mail*, 29 March 1926
16. *The Sunday Post*, 28 March 1926
17. *Athletic News*, 29 March 1926
18. *Yorkshire Evening Post*, 21 April 1926
19. *The Star Green 'Un*, 12 June 1926
20. *Athletic News*, 26 April 1926

Chapter Sixteen

Football That Kills

'A BARSON STORY
One of the best stories told about Frank
Barson really does not concern him all.
Manchester United have a reserve centre-
half who was an even bigger fellow than
the senior side captain, and who was very
surprised one afternoon when a referee
several times addressed him as "Frank",
finally threatening to send him off. Then it
dawned on George Haslam, who went to
the official and said: "Look here, my name
is Haslam, not Barson."' **Shields Daily**
News, Friday, 4 March 1927.

IN OCTOBER 1926 Frank Barson penned an article for the *Liverpool Echo* in which he suggested that the offside rule change had reduced the number of stoppages in the game and thus increased the pace and thus the pressure on players. Spectators got more football for their money and also got more goals. However: 'More than once I have had this feeling that already the game is suffering a bit and in a way which is seldom thought about owing to the break-neck pace and the ding-dong nature of the battle. I have played in some matches out of which a great deal of the life went long before the end. Some of the players were "finished" so far as effective running about was concerned. The spectators may declare that the players ought to be able to go through the whole of 90 minutes no matter how fast the pace. I would like him to try a modern up and down game on a muddy ground. He would find that it wasn't so easy to keep up the pace as it seems on the face of things.'[1]

Whether the pace was killing Barson or not, the truth was that his body was feeling the strain and his injuries would now play an increasingly debilitating part in his career. During the 1926/27 season, he would only play 21 games – half the total of league matches possible – and would never manage to string together more than three games at a stretch. He was also playing in a side that was not being replenished. *All Sports Weekly* made the point in September beneath the headline 'Big Profit, Small Return'. Manchester United had taken £22,000 through the turnstiles in two years, 'Yet the United do not furnish the football and the personalities of the game which such loyal support demands.'[2]

Hughie Gallacher was cited as a player the club might have gone for but hadn't. Just to emphasise the point, he turned on an exhibition when United visited St James' Park on 11 September that only rubbed salt into the wound.

During the game, *Athletic News*'s correspondent wrote, 'Northumbrian' wrote that Barson strove hard but,

'Barson at play'

> How many different roles he filled in the first half while always at his post as pivot it would be idle to calculate. Time and again on Saturday, by the exercise of his craft and foresight, McPherson and his line were simply asked to put the finishing touches to Barson's cleverly conceived designs, only to render them abortive by wild shooting and other examples of ineptitude ...

Gallagher, however, 'is a priceless asset to Newcastle ... the light which eclipsed all others ...'[3]

When Barson was fit and in the team, however, they generally performed as in a 2-0 victory over Cardiff City in late September. Cymro in *Athletic News*:

THE MASTER MIND

Of the individual performances of the victors, none can be compared with that of Barson. He was the mastermind behind a good team, and almost every movement of the forwards could be directly traced to his initiative. It might be said with truth that he found the task of subduing so easy that he devoted most of his time to evolving and executing forward movements. In any case he directed their operations with consummate skill, and undoubtedly ensured his side's victory.[4]

Matters were not proceeding happily off the pitch, however, and in October there came the shock announcement that manager John Chapman was to be suspended by the Football Association for the remainder of the season for 'improper conduct', although what those words meant no one, not even Chapman, would explain.

Football historians have delved and discovered that Chapman had been queried by club directors earlier in the year concerning a relatively small amount of money (no more than £56 apparently) which had either gone missing or been misdirected.

Chapman had offered to pay the money back (he was, in fact, an extremely wealthy man by means of a substantial inheritance) and the United board had accepted the offer.

However, a vengeful club director had informed the FA of the issue and after a couple of special hearings Chapman was suspended. He declared in a newspaper article that he had nothing on his conscience. Manchester

United footballer writer Alf Clarke referred to the incident many years later, stating that Chapman had told him all about it, that it had 'involved a player' and that Chapman could easily have cleared himself.

Instead, he resigned and, after an unsuccessful application to manage Leeds United, left the game entirely. He later managed and invested in greyhound racing and moved to Plymouth.

Whether the 'player' referred to was Barson is impossible to tell, although his two months without pay must have hit him hard.

According to Jack Smith, one of Barson's team-mates at the time, Barson was certainly paid 'extra' for his appearances. Barson would walk into the United dressing room prior to changing for a game and would put a hand on to a shelf in search of a package before he took his coat off. 'In the package was a few extra bob he got extra because he was half the team. One day there was no package and he said to the trainer, "Where's the doin's? I'm not taking my bloody coat off till I get it."'[5]

Had it been illegal payments, however, the FA would have certainly pursued Barson as well, which they didn't. Barson certainly liked Chapman and his departure added to the sense that maybe it was time for Barson's top-line career to also come to an end.

A week after Chapman's exit, Clarence Hilditch was appointed player-manager and Walter Crickmer was appointed secretary – a post the latter would fill until his death in the Munich Air Crash some 30-odd years later.

Barson scored in a 2-1 win over Aston Villa in October but it was the start of an injury/illness-prone period when he would miss eight of the next 11 games. He managed to return for the two Christmas games against Spurs. In a 1-1 draw at White Hart Lane he impressed: 'The other big man on the Manchester side was Barson – a real centre-half-back and a real captain, coming back to show his best form. His tackling was often too good and quick for the home forwards, and when the ball was in the air it was his five times out of six.'[6] And on New Year's Day 1927 he oversaw a 5-0 defeat of Sheffield United, scoring with a header, 'that dazed him and called for the trainer's attention ...'

Then came three season-defining matches: a triple header, as it were, as United tried in vain to eliminate Reading from the FA Cup. During the first match, Reading lost Dougall, their outside-right, with a broken leg courtesy of a hefty tackle by half-back Bennion. Almost immediately they scored to take the lead, but in the celebratory aftermath Reading's McConnell rushed up to Barson and, 'made an offensive gesture in Barson's face'. He was promptly sent off. Reading's nine men then battled through for a draw, United equalising in the very last minute.

The second match, at Villa Park, ended 2-2 and on 17 January Reading at last succeeded in eliminating United, scoring in the last minute to earn a 2-1 victory. The games had been significant for Barson in that he had found himself being out-played and dominated by a young centre-half who some observers saw as the next England 'pivot'.

'Outside Right', for the *Derby Daily Telegraph*, who usually sang Barson's praises, while enthusing over the victory of 'humble and unfashionable' Reading, had been struck by the performance of Alf Messer.

MESSER FOR ENGLAND

Here is a centre-half, tall, strongly built, possessing fine speed and stamina, a player who is right in the prime of his manhood at 25 years of age. Opposing him, on United's side, was Frank Barson, who, two or three years ago, was without a peer in the realm of centre-half-backs. It was a wonderful opportunity for making a direct comparison, for the man who can compare with Barson, even today, is a player worth going a long way see. Well, this player Messer came out of the comparison with flying colours, and if there is a better pivot in the land today then I would like to be led to the ground where he next performs.

MESSER'S POWER

Barson, although the best of the visiting half-backs, did not dominate the game in the manner which he is accustomed to do and in comparison compared unfavourably with Messer, who finished the game as he began.[7]

Barson felt that Reading had a good chance to win the cup, possessing as they did 'the strength and stamina, together with some of the style of the formidable Barnsley cup winners of 1911/12, although, as a team, perhaps they are not quite so vigorous'. Messer, he conceded, was one of the best centre-halves in Britain. (In the event,

Messer never became a star nor played for England. He featured in 271 matches for Reading and scored 18 goals between 1923 and 1929. He signed for Tottenham Hotspur in 1930 but his career stalled and he eventually joined Bournemouth & Boscombe, where he made a further ten appearances and where he finally ended his playing career.)

Barson managed to turn out against Aston Villa in February at Villa Park, where the 35,000 crowd, according to the *Athletic News*'s 'Brum', 'seemed to take it too seriously for they spent a not inconsiderable part of the afternoon hooting Barson, once the idol of the same crowd ... Barson certainly did not play a docile game but without exonerating him from all blame in certain incidents it seemed to me the crowd were disposed to overrate his vigour ...'[8]

March saw him suffering with flu before returning for the last eight games, of which they won two and drew six to finish 15th. In April, who should arrive as Manchester United's new manager, but ex-referee Herbert Bamlett. Apparently, according to Barson, they were able to share a joke about their last strange meeting.

Season 1927/28 would be Barson's last for the club. He would make just 11 appearances, ten of them coming before the end of November. In September he again ventured into print (*The Glut of Goals*) suggesting that the all-out attacking tendencies of First Division clubs was really only due to 'early season enthusiasm'. Soon, however, clubs realise that they are giving too many goals away and rein in, particularly when the grounds start to get hard, 'like concrete'. One could almost hear him wincing, as he sustained a lower-spinal injury early in the season, but not before he'd curbed one of the rising stars of the game, Middlesbrough's high-scoring centre-forward George Camsell. In a 3-0 defeat at Old Trafford, Camsell found Barson all over him from the start and was, 'unable to make a pass to the wing or single-handed raid on goal'.

In late November, Barson led United to a 5-1 win in his benefit match against, inevitably, Aston Villa. The Seer in *Athletic News* wrote:

> Frank Barson celebrated his benefit match playing a particularly clever game and helping Manchester United to beat his old colleagues Aston Villa by five goals to one. He showed the football of which he is capable. It was only now and again that he really booted the ball, and practically all through it was only with a movement of the head, or tap with the side of the foot, that got his forwards on the move.[9]

Billy Walker, unable (and probably thankful not) to play in the match due to injury, wrote:

> Among our Manchester opponents will be Frank Barson, who used to wear Villa colours. If there is any particular match to which Frank looks forward to with special interest it is that with Villa. More than once he has told me that he would sooner help to beat Villa than any other team in the world, and when we meet United. Frank plays as though he means it. He neither spares himself – nor us. When

with Villa he was easily the greatest centre-half in the British Isles and I have yet to see his equal. I would much sooner have Frank on my side than against us.[10]

The following week, United lost 4-0 at Burnley and once again there were uncomfortable comparisons made: *Athletic News*'s Harricus wrote,

One had the opportunity of comparing the merits of two great centre-half-backs, but there was no comparison, for Barson was simply dwarfed by Jack Hill, who played one of his best games, whereas Barson seemed to be somewhat discouraged by his own lack of success. Hill was equally conspicuous as attacker and defender, and, in confirmation of his attacking abilities, I need only state that he obtained the best goal of the match by a brilliant individual effort.[11]

Barson's spinal injury would now keep him out until March when he reappeared for the very last time in United's colours, at Portsmouth. There is something both sad and at the same time typically defiant about his last first-class performance:

Barson, however, was reported fit again and resumed his old position as pivot and captain. For 20 minutes he set his men a fine example and backed his attack cleverly ... Then came calamity for the United. Barson and Johnston both ran into

Manchester United's FA Cup nemesis

position to head a dropping ball. There was not an
opponent near and not the slightest danger. Barson
advanced for it and Johnston retreated. Had either

shouted 'right' or, failing this, for both had eyes on the ball, had a colleague given quick advice, a collision would have been avoided, but Barson's nose came into contact with the back of Johnston's head and the centre-half-back collapsed.

He was led off the field bleeding profusely, but was soon back again, heavily plastered. For a time he struggled in his usual position with great gallantry, but he was obviously in pain and went to outside-left. He retired from the game at the interval, when it was found that he had broken his nose.[12]

Endnotes

1. *Liverpool Echo*, 30 October 1926
2. *All Sports Weekly*, 25 September 1926
3. *Athletic News*, 13 September 1926
4. *Athletic News*, Monday, 27 September 1926
5. Harry Godwin, Manchester City Scout, *The Guardian*, 19 March 1980
6. *Athletic News*, Monday, 27 December 1926
7. *Derby Daily Telegraph*, 22 January 1927
8. *Athletic News*, 21 February 1927
9. *Athletic News*, Monday, 21 November 1927
10. *Sports Argus*, Saturday, 19 November 1927
11. *Athletic News*, 28 November 1927
12. *Athletic News*, 19 March 1928

Chapter Seventeen

Justice for Frank?

'FREE TRANSFER FOR BARSON
Frank Barson, the Manchester United
centre-half-back, who has been given a free
transfer, said he was agreeably surprised.
They had paid a big price for him, he said,
but he felt, without boasting, he had repaid
them. Examined by a specialist, he was
found to be as good as ever, and should
not be surprised if the English Selection
Committee honoured him the second time ...'
Northern Whig, Saturday, 5 May 1928.

DURING INTERWAR close seasons, readers of the
Thomson's Weekly News could keep track of their football
favourites via letters written by the latter to the editor.
In July, Barson give a brief glimpse of his activities and
his destination.

On the Bowling Green

    Major,

    Don't ask me what I think of the close season! I couldn't truthfully tell you but I will say I have been fortunate in having my former clubmates Jack Silcock and Harry Thomas for company. We have put in many strenuous hours on the bowling green and while I haven't had much success with the woods I hope I am good enough for my opponents! As you know I have changed my camp and am just wondering who I will meet at Watford …

    All the best, Yours Sincerely, Frank Barson.

    Watford FC[1]

Watford certainly was a surprise move for Barson, who appeared at that moment to have many possible choices as to where to hang his football hat/boots. He was 37 years old, and apparently fighting fit again. Watford, meanwhile, had just been re-elected to the Football League Third Division South. They were also in some financial distress. In August it was reported that they were having trouble paying the council rates, and that the club was looking into the idea of merging with a greyhound racing organisation who would pay £2,000 a year in rent – a 'salvation' for the club, apparently.

The *Derby Daily Telegraph* reporter explained one of the reasons why, despite their financial woes, the club ended up signing Barson:

Another famous player, with Yorkshire associations, who has changed hands with a free transfer is Frank Barson, and he is to put Watford on the royal road to promotion next season. His transfer is really the story of two Franks – Pagnam and Barson. The now former manager at Watford, as well as being mine host of a well-known hotel, was also one of the most popular players that ever kicked ball in the centre-forward position. He and Frank Barson are old friends. Therein you have the secret why Barson has gone to Watford.[2]

Watford manager Pagnam was an unconventional character with a colourful past. The son of a bank manager, he made a name for himself as a robust Liverpool forward, and in 1917 he gave evidence in a libel case in connection with a notorious Manchester United v Liverpool match-fixing scandal, testifying that he had been illegally approached but refused to participate. He'd signed for Arsenal in 1919, and during his time at Highbury had found time to become the manager of the nearby Finsbury Park cinema. He scored prolifically for the Gunners for a season or two before moving on to Cardiff in 1921, a move the didn't work out. He then signed for Watford and scored 74 goals in 157 games before being appointed manager in 1926. He was – according to a Watford historian – a non-conformist whose quirky personality was not universally popular.

While still a player, he had to apologise to the directors for behaviour which had been the subject of complaint by his colleagues, and he retained his individual streak after taking charge.

Many years later George Jewett, who played under Pagnam, recalled him as 'barmy, a bad-principled man, didn't get respect'. Jewett also revealed that Frank Barson had told him that he was 'finished' when he signed for Watford but had got manager Fred Pagnam drunk as a means towards securing the engagement for which Barson had received £1,000 from Watford chairman Kilby on signing.

Alcohol was clearly a key factor in Barson's move. Pagnam had set himself up as a pub landlord (of the nearby Swan Hotel, Rickmansworth) and within a month or so Barson was making a move to do likewise.

Benskin's Brewery was keen for him to take the licence of Watford's King William IV pub in the High Street and applications were made to the local magistrates. Barson clearly saw Watford as his final stop on his long football journey from Grimesthorpe.

At the same time, he was by no means finished on the pitch. In his debut match at Crystal Palace he was cautioned early on in the game and, ominously perhaps, when the Watford player Joe Davison was later sent off, the referee reportedly said, 'Off you go, Barson.'

Watford lost the match 3-0 but drew the next and won twice in September, with Barson scoring. In the second of those, a Coventry player was struck on the head and played on in a semi-conscious state before collapsing, and in the following game Watford's Warner broke a collar bone and left after 25 minutes. Against Plymouth,

Barson conceded a penalty as Watford lost 2-0 before the calamity of the Fulham game.

Reports of the previous Watford games, albeit generally skimpy, suggest he was his usual dominant and skilful self and a class above both his team-mates and opponents. He controlled his new team just as he had his various Manchester United squads. However, some unease must have been stirring in official circles.

The referee appointed for the fateful Fulham match was a Mr W.E. Russell, a man of some 20 years' experience and who was considered to be a refereeing 'strong man', someone to be called upon when trouble threatened. A First World War hero, the recipient of a Military Medal, an outstanding personal characteristic was the 'irrevocability' of his decisions, while he was noted for his coolness and firmness in controlling 'difficult' matches.

> He came into special prominence during the last few seasons, being given special assignments by the FA when trouble threatened in certain South Wales matches, he being at the last moment selected to take charge of games when a fear of unruliness asserted itself.
>
> Again in the trouble between Tottenham Hotspur and Arsenal two seasons ago he was appointed to take control after being assigned an ordinary routine match far distant from the Metropolis.[3]

Some years prior, Russell had received the approval of another referee who'd featured heavily in Barson's career.

At a public meeting, in the presence of Russell and Fleming, the famous international forward, Jack Howcroft declared that Swindon possessed as brilliant a referee as it did an inside-forward, and prophesied that which has now matured, viz., that Russell would shortly he selected for the premier honour among referees.[4]

Russell was awarded the 1924 FA Cup Final, which was, in fact, a big surprise apparently, and said to be owing to the FA's desire for more control to be exercised over its showpiece event.

As ever, however, professional players were not quite as enamoured of Mr Russell. Rather than quelling dissent, his decisions sometimes caused it. Tempers could become frayed on the pitch when W.E. Russell of Swindon was officiating. 'A bossy-boots by nature, Russell treated the players like errant schoolboys and, once the game was in motion, he made a habit never to venture beyond the centre-circle.'[5]

Without venturing too far into conspiracy theory territory, it might appear rather odd that Russell would suddenly be given a Third Division South match to control, but no surprise that he would send Barson off, as one of his colleagues had apparently been intent on doing in Barson's very first match.

It mustn't be thought, however, that everyone felt sorry for Barson. George Jewett – considered a reliable first-hand witness who was playing when the infamous sending-off occurred – also recalled that at half-time Watford director Jeffs went to the changing room and

told Barson he should be ashamed of himself, whereupon
Barson grabbed Jeffs (apparently a very small man) by the
neck and threatened him.

Nevertheless, after the first petition calling for Barson's sending-off to be rescinded had been ceremoniously (perhaps even gleefully) burned by FA Secretary Lewis, a second one was raised by the Supporters' Club, this time for supporters across the country. It ultimately bore some 15,000 signatures and was equally futile. Whether the FA burned this one as well is not known. They simply stated that those who signed it did not know the facts and thus declined to re-open the enquiry.

There were rumours that the Watford team would refuse to play if Barson was not reinstated but Pagnam soon quashed that idea. 'There is absolutely no foundation for such rumour,' he said to a 'Post' representative. 'We are playing Luton tomorrow at home and expect a big gate. The team will definitely turn out.'[6]

Thus the football caravan moved on, leaving Barson by the wayside. As if to rub salt into the wound, the man Watford turned to as their new manager would be none other than Neil McBain.

Though a severe blow to him (his public house licence application was quietly withdrawn some months into the new year), his treatment by the FA raised issues of fairness that saw a small but significant change occur in the way it handled disciplinary cases.

The FA had been caught rather unawares, in a way, when its high-handed behaviour had not been as readily accepted as it once might. Burning the Watford petition was deemed particularly offensive, even though it had been the hapless Watford mayor's idea, and there was particular unease at the revelation that, once such a decision was made, there was no appeal allowed.

Strangely enough (although given his close interest in such affairs, perhaps not so strange) Barson himself had raised the issue some four years previously in an article he'd penned entitled 'Players' Court of Appeal'.

'Under the present system of "trying players by correspondence" there is far too much time wasted. Often it is six or seven weeks after a player has been reported for an offence that his punishment is announced, and during that time it invariably happens that letters have passed between the FA, the referee, the club, and the player – backwards and forwards – stating their own cases and rebutting or acquiescing in the statements made by other parties.

'The system is old-fashioned and out of date. But there is another far more important aspect to this method of trying players for alleged offences. While I agree that there has been a better class of player attracted to football as a profession since the rate of wages was increased, there are still very many players who could do themselves and their case far greater justice were they able to give evidence by word of mouth. Many players can speak well and clearly, but many of them are not nearly so happy when it comes to putting their case in writing.'

He referred to recent cases where players had not been sent off but had been suspended (a premonition, perhaps, of what would happen to him?). In those cases, 'The blow has descended out of the darkness, as it were, and seems somewhat out of place in these days of enlightenment.'

He ended his article suggesting that, 'True justice is never a hardship.'[7]

At the time he had received some support from C.E. Sutcliffe, who'd emphasised that the argument that personal hearings would cost too much money was deeply flawed. Players looked to lose a great deal of money and 'justice should be seen to be done'.[8]

This time round, the pressure on the FA to alter the system increased. The Herts and Essex County FA, clearly responding to the Barson case and its handling by the FA, put forward a proposal at the FA's Annual General Meeting that summer to put an end to 'trials by correspondence' and in spite of determined opposition from some of the game's legendary administrators, an overwhelming majority carried it.

> On this particular matter it would seem that the governing authorities had not realised how bitterly opposed to the old system were the rank and file. For years clubs and players suffered from a sense of injustice, and it is surprising action was delayed so long.[9]

At a time when the Players' Union was experiencing something of a revival, with new offices being established in Manchester and a new, determined secretary appointed in Jimmy Fay, Barson's treatment had touched a chord and thus contributed, albeit indirectly, to a significant change in the quasi-legal status of the professional footballer. Barson would no doubt have been pleased by such an outcome – a rare incidence of retribution for the many wrongs he considered, rightly or wrongly, had been done to him.

Endnotes

1. *Thomson's Weekly News*, July 1928
2. *Sheffield/Derby Daily Telegraph*, 19 May 1928
3. *Birmingham Daily Gazette*, 1 April 1924
4. *Birmingham Daily Gazette*, 2 April 1924
5. Geraint H. Jenkins, *Proud to be a Swan – The History of Swansea City FC* (Tal-y-bont, Wales: Y Lolfa, 2013)
6. *Watford Observer*, 20 October 1928
7. *Derby Daily Telegraph*, 24 March 1923
8. *Liverpool Echo*, 20 January 1923
9. *Sheffield Daily Telegraph*, 5 June 1929

Chapter Eighteen

Barson the Roamer

'BELFAST CELTIC AND BARSON
Belfast Celtic are in touch with Frank Barson,
the former Manchester United, Aston Villa, and
England centre-half, who was with Hartlepools
United last season, says the Daily Express. If
terms can be agreed the deal will be completed
before the weekend.' **Hartlepool Northern Daily**
Mail, Tuesday, 15 July 1930.

'While at Rhyl I met my old colleague Frank
Barson who is now associated with Rhyl
Athletic. Frank looked very fit and well
and they tell me that though he has slowed
down a bit he is playing almost as well as
ever. We talked of the old days and he wound
up by assuring me that Aston Villa was the
best club in the world ...' **Sports Argus,**
16 January 1932.

FOR SOMEONE who had caused so much trouble when at Aston Villa concerning his right to live in Grimesthorpe, it's ironic that Barson would now spend the next 20 years or so traipsing the length and breadth of England and Wales in search of a secure football home. What he found for the most part were short-term options relying on connections and old friendships, meeting people from his past like ships passing in the night.

From Watford to Hartlepool is some 250 miles as the crow flies, but that was where he found himself within a month of leaving Watford, living in a narrow rented house a few hundred yards from Hartlepool's Victoria ground. The small port town was suffering from heavy unemployment at the time and the club was struggling in the Football League Division Three (North), and, in fact, had finished second from bottom in the preceding year.

The connection was his old Barnsley trainer, Will Norman, who was Hartlepool manager. After leaving Barnsley for Huddersfield with Arthur Fairclough, he'd joined Blackpool as manager before rejoining Fairclough at Leeds. When Leeds were relegated, he took over at Hartlepool but would die there in 1931.

At a gathering of the team in late August, Hartlepool's mayor had a word with Barson, who expressed himself as very contented with his new quarters and added, 'I think I have got with me a likely lot of players who will put every ounce of energy into their work.'

Barson was joined by an old United colleague, Albert Pape, but sadly was soon injured, before suffering a bout of appendicitis that required a sojourn in hospital. He managed just nine games, during which time he was taken to the supporters' hearts. It was thus a shock when he was let go in April 1930.

> Frank Barson, the old Manchester United, Barnsley, etc. centre-half, has worked such a change at Hartlepool since he went there from Watford as player-manager that it is hard to understand his reason for leaving at the expiration of this season. The 'Pools have enjoyed probably their most successful season since they became a league side and Barson's tuition has been invaluable to the younger players.[1]

Barson was now reduced to placing an advert in *Athletic News* in mid-April 1930: 'Frank Barson. Open for Season 1930/31; sound and fit; free transfer as agreed.'

Offers arrived and in July he travelled to Wigan, another town suffering from industrial decline, as was Wigan Borough FC, a club on the brink of extinction. In fact, it was to be the Borough's last full season as a Football League club and Barson would make 19 appearances for them. His final appearance was unscheduled as such, against Accrington Stanley on Boxing Day 1930, when he was sent off in the 83rd minute for allegedly jumping on an opponent.

'It was reported that in Wigan's match with Accrington on Boxing Day Barson was alleged to have jumped in a dangerous manner at an opponent and to have used obscene language to the referee, Mr. T. Greaves, of Burslem, after being ordered off.

'The commission are satisfied that the conduct of both teams in the match did not reflect any credit upon the players concerned.'[2] Barson was fined £5 and suspended until the end of March.

He actually turned out for Wigan in February in a Manchester Senior Cup match against Manchester

United, but by the second half of the season gates were pitiful and the Wigan club was in serious danger of folding. Barson was inevitably Wigan's highest-paid player and in an effort to stabilise the club's deteriorating finances he was let go in June 1931. Wigan Borough itself limped on until October that year when it ceased to exist, its players appealing to the Players' Union as their wages were unforthcoming.

By then, Frank Barson was 70 miles away, on the Welsh coast, ever enthusiastic, training for his new player-coach role with Rhyl Athletic, where he would remain until his contract was terminated in March 1935.

Rhyl were members of the Birmingham and District League and an ambitious club, boasting a supporters' club membership of some 26,000. Though he was no longer playing weekly, Barson was still able to hit the headlines. In October 1932 a local derby against Bangor erupted into an all-out fight.

> Attack after attack was launched upon the Bangor goal and it was during one of these, after Kyle had saved from Durban, that all the players, except Roberts and Fairhurst, Rhyl's right-back and goalkeeper, congregated in the Bangor goalmouth and a free fight ensued. It was impossible to see who was to blame, and the climax was reached when Barson and Durban (Rhyl) and Roy, an ex-Rhyl player, of Bangor, were ordered off the field, and Drain Bangor's inside-left, was carried off unconscious. The crowd were surprised that Referee Tilston of Chester thought fit to

include Barson in the offending players, because he appeared to be the only one trying to restore order.[3]

At an FA commission in Chester on 29 October 1932 the charge against Barson actually failed, while other players received heavy fines and suspension.

The following year he hit the headlines again, breaking two ribs and a toe but carrying on playing, while in April 1933 he and the team were again in the news. Having two fixtures to fulfil 100 miles apart, the club paid for the players to take an aeroplane:

> At 3.30pm they will be at Stafford to play a Birmingham League game and at 6.30pm they will turn out at Bangor for the final of the North Wales Challenge Cup. No car or train could get the team from Stafford to Bangor in time so the players will be rushed from the Midlands to their North Wales destination in a specially chartered aeroplane. This only the second time in football history that a team has travelled by air to fulfil a fixture in England.[4]

His Welsh experience came to an end, however, in March 1935 when the club let him go in a cost-cutting exercise. He was now 44 and hadn't played for a season due to injuries.

Within three months he re-surfaced as the trainer of Stourbridge, but then came an unlikely but welcome offer: a return to Aston Villa.

It was a time of turmoil at Villa Park. Barson arrived as a youth coach in July but soon afterwards Villa manager Jimmy McMullan resigned as the club toppled towards Division Two. Barson was then promoted to head coach and team trainer – a position that Billy Walker, then manager of Sheffield Wednesday and widely tipped to take over at Villa, advised the club to offer him. Assisted by Herbert Bourne, who'd played with Barson in Villa's FA Cup win in 1920, Barson was now the club's manager in all but name, although the major decisions were now taken by the club's hierarchy.

In August, following Villa's inevitable relegation, the club took the daring step of employing Jimmy Hogan as their new manager. Hogan was considered a revolutionary football thinker, having spent most of his career on the continent working with pioneering football coaches such as Austria's Hugo Meisl. A believer in coaching and in youth schemes, things generally given a cold shoulder in the English game, he and Barson made a strange pair, Barson ostensibly representing all that Hogan rejected.

However, Hogan immediately spotted that the old warrior was the perfect man to take charge of Villa's Colts team, based at the club's Alexander Grounds, Perry Bar. Barson would produce, it was hoped, the future stars for Villa; in 1937, he was also put in charge of what was termed Hogan's Juniors, being a team of youngsters aged 11 to 16 from whom Villa's future playing strength was to be largely recruited.

Barson appears to have embraced Hogan's philosophy, even to the extent of accompanying Hogan on a trip to the Carnegie Physical Training College at Leeds in July 1939 for the fifth annual Summer School, where all the new ideas and philosophies were discussed and demonstrated. What Barson felt about Hogan's scheme to prevent brain damage to footballers when heading the ball (to replace footballs every 15 minutes during a match) is not known.

The Second World War ended Hogan's Villa experiments, however, but not before he managed to lift Villa back into Division One. Barson, too, found his contract terminated once again and for a time he was completely out of football, finding employment as a farm bailiff in Worcestershire.

In 1947, however, his old footballing connections led him to his last full-time post, that of trainer at Swansea Town, then in Division Three (South). The Swansea manager at the time was one Haydn Green, who'd played for both Manchester United and Aston Villa just after the First World War, and thus knew Barson well.

Green would depart in 1948 and Scotsman Billy McCandless replaced him, Swansea gaining promotion in season 1948/49 to Division Two where they would remain for Barson's stint as trainer. McCandless commented, 'Barson is a most useful man here. We see eye to eye on how things should be run and that means a lot.'

Swansea, though a Second Division club, would possess some truly great Welsh players during Barson's years there, including Trevor Ford, Ivor and Len Allchurch, Mel Charles, Terry Medwin, Cliff Jones and Mel Nurse. (There was also a player on the Swansea books during those years called Rory Keane ...)

Barson still managed to get his name into the papers, however. In November 1952, during a hard 1-1 draw with Leicester City, he was spotted on the touchline with six footballs. As fast as the Leicester defence hit a ball out of the ground in order to waste time, Barson (yelling 'Keep it going!') booted another onto the pitch with a runner retrieving 'lost' balls from the street outside.

The following year there occurred his last encounter with a referee. The *Western Mail* reported an, 'unusual touchline incident: Early in the second half, Mr P. Martin, the referee, warned Swansea Town trainer Frank Barson after he dipped the ball into his bucket of water. The referee wiped it dry with a towel.'[5]

Swansea players of the time recalled Barson in various ways, some preferring to emphasise the caricature. Tom Kiley, who was at the club for 11 years, making 129 appearances, dismissed Barson thus: 'We had Frank Barson as a trainer. He was a man who hated me because I wasn't dirty enough. He was a blunt Barnsley lad and said, "Ee by gum, if I were your size when I were playing I have a graveyard of centre-forwards all to meself." The edict was that if it moved – kick it, if it doesn't move – kick it until it does move. Get it down field that's all he ever said.'[6]

International half-back Roy Paul, a player whose career was also somewhat controversial at times (he was one of the famous Bogota Bandits, British players who broke their contracts to go to South America in search of better terms) felt there was much more to Barson than just 'kicking it'.

> Barson was nearing 60 when I first met him. I thought at first that he might be one of the know-all old-timers always telling you how good it was in the old days. I soon dismissed that idea. Out came Barson in training kit to prove he could still nip smartly in a sprint. He explained to me quite simply, almost modestly, 'They used to call me the centre-forwards graveyard, Roy.'
>
> I can well believe it. He used to keep a little notebook detailing every flick, feint and foul

opponents had pulled when playing against him. They never did it a second time because Barson read and re-read his little storehouse of soccer knowledge as religiously as if it was a bible. This tungsten steel character explained the need for strong tackling half-backs and would say to me: 'Don't break their legs Roy … but let them know you are there when you go into a tackle. Don't push out a tentative toe, like a man testing the Serpentine on a cold and frosty morning. Put your weight into the tackle. Make it bite. You must go in hard and fairly to take the ball off the other fellow.'[7]

Barson took Paul out onto the training ground for hour after hour, demonstrating tackling and positional play. At one point he showed Paul the scars on his eyebrows: 'That's what centre-forwards did to you Roy with their back headers. They could zip your eye brows open as though with a surgeon's scalpel if you let them get in first.'

Barson retired in 1954 on the grounds of ill-health. His home was now in Birmingham, which had necessitated his having to stay in lodgings in Swansea. However, in October he was back in the game once more, spending two days a week training players of Birmingham League side Lye Town. Two years on, he stepped away from the training pitch completely.

He spent his retirement years living not too far from the Aston Villa ground, the club with which he'd won his one and only major medal. He would occasionally be interviewed in the local Birmingham paper, generally to provide some typically forthright outburst concerning the sad state of the modern game ('Football can be learned ONLY ON THE FIELD. Not from chalk marks on a blackboard ...') and players in general ('Players should be paid what they're worth, that's the big plea of today's footballers and I agree. But most of them would be picking up pennies not pounds!').

Such articles didn't do him or his legacy much justice, but there was always that sense of mischief about his pronouncements, as though he only half believed them himself.

By the mid-1960s he'd been all but forgotten by the game in general, although not by Villa fans who saw him regularly at home games. When he turned 70, they decorated a bar in the Holte Hotel, Aston – his local – with pictures of him. It was, he said, 'A day to remember'.

He revelled in Villa's 1957 cup success over his other old club, Manchester United, but Villa were soon struggling in to league just as they had done when he had been brought in the save them back in 1919. In fact, almost exactly 50 years on, the two clubs he had striven to return to former glories would experience contrasting fortunes: Manchester United would be the first English team to win the European Cup, while Villa would fall into the Third Division.

Barson would not witness the latter sad event. In August 1968 he died aged 77. In 2007 his precious FA Cup medal was bought by an anonymous collector for £7,680...

Afterword

IN OCTOBER 1928, when Barson's Watford woes had first descended upon him, 'Bantam', in the *Midland Daily Telegraph*, wrote:

> I cannot help the conviction that, whatever the faults Barson showed, he has been rather unkindly treated by followers of the game. He has always been something of a stormy petrel and the attention he drew unto himself has been rather inimical to his welfare. It was like fanning a flame that was always there. Barson, at any rate, has one good quality apart from his ability. He was always ready to take over other players' troubles and I have seen him incur the displeasure of a crowd and sometimes earn an admonition from the referee because he abrogated to himself the right to retaliate for a victimised colleague. He has been unwise to do so but in his hour of depression no one will be unchivalrous enough to begrudge him this little commendation.[8]

Endnotes

1. *The People*, 27 April 1930
2. *Northern Daily Mail*, 9 January 1931
3. *Belfast Telegraph*, 21 October 1932
4. *Liverpool Echo*, 25 April 1933
5. *Western Mail*, 20 April 1953
6. Tom Kiley interview, 2011-12
7. Roy Paul, *The Red Dragon of Wales*, 1956, pp. 21-22
8. *Midland Daily Telegraph*, 20 October 1928

Epilogue

Barson and the
Men in Black

FOOTBALL, IT seemed, felt the need to react to Frank Barson's arrival in the world in April 1891. Within a few months of his birth, as if anticipating many of the problems he would soon be causing, the game's administrators, the Football Association, took the precaution of creating the modern referee.

In the early years of the sport it was assumed that disputes could be adequately settled by discussion between 'gentlemen' players who would never deliberately commit a foul. Initially there existed two umpires, one per team. When contentious moments arrived, the umpires would discuss the matter between themselves and try to come to an agreement, but if they couldn't then the issue would be referred to the 'referee' who was keeping time and he would have the deciding vote.

However, as play became more competitive, the need for more 'hands-on' officials grew, and in 1891 the Football Association agreed to a re-structuring of the rules of the game. Now the referee became the dominant official, entering the field of play while umpires became linesmen.

Below are some of the men in black with whom Barson interacted during his long career.

Charles Clegg, who died in 1937 at the age of 87, by which time he was known as 'the great old man of football' having served the Football Association for over 51 years. A first-class referee, his engagements included two FA Cup finals, 1882 and 1892, as well as the England against Scotland matches in 1886 and 1893. He first suggested the umpire's flag in 1874 and presented Barson's favourite team Barnsley with the FA Cup in 1912.

J.T. Howcroft of Bolton, who made his name on the track as a racing cyclist and remained actively interested in the management and government of cycling. He became a linesman in 1898, and eventually a referee for the Lancashire Combination. After one season he was admitted to the league list and despite the 'claims of business' continued to 'officiate with distinction in important matches'. He was secretary of the Manchester, Bolton and Bury and the Lancashire Referees' Associations. He refereed the 1920 FA Cup Final and had a long career in football journalism in the 1930s, always referred to as 'the famous' referee.

W.T. Russell, born in Swindon, who turned his attention to refereeing in 1904 when he took his first match at the

Swindon Recreation Ground. He was soon refereeing in the Wiltshire League and the Western League. Placed on the Southern League list in 1908, he made rapid headway, being given a semi-final in the Amateur Cup, and he officiated when Newcastle United defeated Chelsea in the FA Cup semi-final of 1910/11. When the war broke out he joined the South Dorsets, took a commission, won the Military Cross and finished his army career with the rank of captain. Returning home during the summer of 1919, he was made a Football League linesman and soon after became a referee. He took the FA Cup Final in 1924.

T.S. Sephton of Derbyshire, who was a teacher all his life. He was headmaster of St James's Church Boys' School (where he'd been educated in the 1880s) for 19 years before retiring in 1940. He was chairman of Derby Football Association in 1936 as well as being an accomplished swimmer – he even accompanied a number of cross-Channel swimmers as they attempted to reach France. He refereed an FA Amateur Cup Final in 1921 between Bishop Auckland and Swindon Victoria and was a regular FA Cup referee. He refereed in the Notts and Derbyshire League before World War One.

Herbert Bamlett, who was born in March 1882 and was only 32 when he refereed the 1914 FA Cup Final between Liverpool and Burnley as well as that year's international between England and Scotland. He later became the manager of Oldham Athletic, Middlesbrough, and Manchester United. He had a breakdown following his departure from Manchester United and lost the sight of one eye. He died in 1941.

William Frederick Bunnell of Preston, who was a commercial traveller by occupation. He was one of the best-known officials on the Football League's list of referees and one with uniformly good reports. 'He is a man who is always prepared to stand by his convictions as witnessed in one of his decisions at Bramall Lane this season when a goalkeeper was ordered off...' He refereed the cup final in 1927 between Cardiff and Arsenal and was president of the Association of Football League Referees and Linesmen in 1932. He handed players who had been cautioned peppermints... 'Bite that and it will keep you quiet...' He retired in 1933 due to ill-health.

Tom Greaves, who was an experienced and capable lower-league referee from the Midlands throughout the 1920s and 30s. He was vice-president of the North Staffs Referees' Club in 1921, and took charge of a charity match in 1936 organised by the Sports Club section of the Burslem Co-operative Society in aid of the North Staffordshire Royal Infirmary, with Stan Matthews and Joe Johnson, then Stoke City players, running the line. He was chairman of the Burslem Christmas Dinner Fund for many years.

Referees were the subject of many stories Barson told about himself. Roy Paul remembered:

'On one occasion Barson went up to protest to the referee, none other than the famous Jack Howcroft, who ruled the players with almost martial efficiency. As Barson started to walk towards him, Howcroft called: "One step nearer Barson and you are…"

"'But I only wanted to ask you the time, ref," butted in Barson with his usual quick wit.

"'Time you carried on with the game, Barson, or you will be in trouble," said Howcroft.'

Books Used

For more on the Players' Union (PFA) history read:
Behind The Glory: 100 Years of the PFA, John Harding (Breedon Books Publishing Company, 2009)

For more on Billy Meredith's life-story read:
Football Wizard: The Story of Billy Meredith, John Harding (Empire Publications, 2014)

For more on The Winning Goal film scripted by Harold Brighouse and starring Frank Barson read:
Staging Life The Story of the Manchester Playwrights, John Harding (Greenwich Exchange), 2018)

50 Years of Football 1884-1934, Frederick Wall (Soccer Books Ltd, 2005)
A Lifetime In Football, Charles Buchan (The Sportsman's Book Club, 1956)
An English Football Internationalists Who's Who, Douglas Lamming (Hutton Press, 1990)
Aston Villa, Peter Morris (The Sportsman's Book Club, 1952)
Aston Villa, The Complete Record, Rob Bishop (DB Publishing, 2010)
Back From The Brink, Justin Blundell (Empire Publications, 2006)
Building Schools for Sheffield 1870 – 1914, Valerie Bayless (The Victorian Society, ALD Print, 2012)
'Heroes of the North: Sport and the Shaping of Regional Identity', Richard Holt in *Sport and Identity in the North of England* Jeff Hill and Jack Williams (eds.) (Keele University Press, 1996)

Inverting the Pyramid, Jonathan Wilson (Orion, 2008)

Lifting The Cup, The Story of Battling Barnsley 1910 – 1912, Mark Metcalf and David Wood (Wharncliffe Books, 2010)

Manchester United A Complete Record 1878 – 1986, Ian Morrison and Alan Shury (Breedon Books, 1986)

Manchester United Football Club, Alf Clarke (Convoy, 1951)

Manchester United, Alf Clarke (Newservice, 1948)

Manchester United. The History of a Great Football Club, Percy Young (Heinemann, 1960)

Oakwell - The Official History of Barnsley F.C., Grenville Firth (Yore Publications, 2012)

Sheffield's East Enders, Keith Farnsworth (Sheffield City Libraries, 1987)

Soccer in the Blood, Billy Walker (Stanley Paul, 1960)

Swifter Than the Arrow: Wilfred Bartrop, Football and War, Peter Holland (Matador, 2009)

The Red Dragon of Wales, Roy Paul (Robert Hale, 1956)

The Who's Who of Barnsley FC, Grenville Firth and David Wood (DB Publishing, 2011)

Watford Season by Season: A Detailed Record of More Than 4,000 Matches from 1881/82, Trefor Jones (T.G.Jones, 1998)

Academic Source

'From Local Hero to National Star?' The changing cultural representation of the professional footballer in England 1945-1985, Joyce Woolridge (A thesis submitted in partial fulfilment of the requirements of the University of Central Lancashire for the degree of Doctor of Philosophy, 2007)

Newspapers and Journals

All Sports Illustrated Weekly
Athletic News
Birmingham Sports Argus
Charles Buchan's Football Monthly, September–December 1956
Derby Daily Telegraph
Football Special
Liverpool Post

Manchester Evening News
Sporting Life
Sports Pictures
The Blizzard
The Daily Mail
The Daily Telegraph
The Guardian
The Times
Thomson's Weekly News
Topical Times
Watford Observer

Life-stories by Barson

The Truth about My Football Troubles by Frank Barson. *Thomson's Weekly News* 2 May – 27 June 1925

Football Meant Trouble by Frank Barson. *Charles Buchan's Football Monthly*. September to December 1956.

The Frank Barson Story. *Sports Argus* 27 August onward 1960

Articles by Barson

Beating Better Teams: *Biggleswade Chronicle*, 4 May 1923

Players Court of Appeal: Reform which will be very acceptable to Professionals, *Derby Daily Telegraph*, 24 March 1923

Centre-forward Trouble: *Liverpool Echo* 24 October 1925

Football That Kills: Games becoming too hard for players to stick to it to the end, *Liverpool Echo*, 30 October 1926

The Men Who Manage: Do they earn their ever-increasing salaries? *Liverpool Echo*, 15 January 1927

Glut of Goals: Is Net-finding now too easy? *Liverpool Echo*, 10 September 1927

Promotion: The tremendous struggle to get to the top class and the risks involved. *Liverpool Echo*, 31 March 1928.

Index

287